# Better Homes and Gardens®

# CHRISTMAS CROSS-STITCH

© Copyright 1987 by Meredith Corporation, Des Moines, Iowa.
All Rights Reserved. Printed in the United States of America.
First Edition. Third Printing, 1988.
Library of Congress Catalog Card Number: 86-62169
ISBN: 0-696-01620 (hard cover)
ISBN: 0-696-01621-4 (trade paperback)

**BETTER HOMES AND GARDENS® BOOKS**

Editor: Gerald M. Knox
Art Director: Ernest Shelton
Managing Editor: David A. Kirchner
Editorial Project Managers: James D. Blume,
    Marsha Jahns, Rosanne Weber Mattson,
    Mary Helen Schiltz

Senior Crafts Books Editor: Joan Cravens
Associate Crafts Books Editors: Liz Porter,
    Beverly Rivers, Sara Jane Treinen

Associate Art Directors: Linda Ford Vermie,
    Neoma Alt West, Randall Yontz
Assistant Art Directors: Lynda Haupert,
    Harijs Priekulis, Tom Wegner
Senior Graphic Designer: Darla Whipple-Frain
Graphic Designers: Mike Burns, Brian Wignall
Art Production: Director, John Berg;
    Associate, Joe Heuer;
    Office Manager, Emma Rediger

President, Book Group: Fred Stines
Vice President, General Manager: Jeramy Lanigan
Vice President, Retail Marketing: Jamie Martin
Vice President, Administrative Services: Rick Rundall

BETTER HOMES AND GARDENS® MAGAZINE
President, Magazine Group: James A. Autry
Vice President, Editorial Director: Doris Eby
Executive Director, Editorial Services: Duane L. Gregg

MEREDITH CORPORATE OFFICERS
Chairman of the Board: E.T. Meredith III
President: Robert A. Burnett
Executive Vice President: Jack D. Rehm

**CHRISTMAS CROSS-STITCH**
Crafts Editor: Sara Jane Treinen
Contributing Editor: Gary Boling
Editorial Project Manager: Rosanne Weber Mattson
Graphic Designer: Sally Cooper
Electronic Text Processor: Paula Forest

**Cover project:** See page 42.

# CONTENTS

# COUNTRY PLAIDS

## THAT SAY MERRY CHRISTMAS

Festive reds and greens stitched into traditional plaid patterns are a combination sure to make your holiday decorating full of enchanting country charm. Here and on the next few pages is an array of Christmas delights—trims, gifts, and accessories. You can stitch them all using the same patterns again and again.

The perky plaid tree trims and star tree topper shown here are sure-fire winners to complement your holiday decorations.

Five separate plaids, worked with red and green embroidery floss, padded and quilted, then accented with pearl cotton braid and a red bow with streamers, make this star topper a shining display of Christmas spirit.

Stitch all six, or more, of the matching 3x3-inch pillow ornaments. Their unique assembly makes them just as pretty on the back side as they are on the front. Complete how-to instructions for all the projects in this chapter begin on page 12.

# COUNTRY PLAIDS

For easy holiday entertaining—whether it's a neighborhood cookie exchange or your fanciest Christmas party—these tabletop accessories will put your guests into the spirit of Christmas.

Stitched with red and green floss onto hardanger, using any one of the plaid patterns, these 12x19-inch place mats are an eye-catching complement to your holiday tableware. You also can work the traditional motifs on purchased napkins, using waste canvas, to complete the set.

This 54x63-inch comfy wool plaid throw and its matching 14x14-inch pillows will add warm and cozy accents to your country Christmas in a guest room or beside the fire.

Using waste canvas, you quickly can stitch the forest of trees across a strip of red woolen fabric. We worked the cross-stitch embellishments with wool yarns, but pearl cotton threads could easily be substituted. Then, complete the throw with a festive wool plaid.

A patchwork of red, green, and plaid borders accentuate the light-colored cross-stitched pillow motifs. Stitch a dozen of these motifs in a twinkling to fill every room in your home with seasonal touches.

# COUNTRY PLAIDS

Youngsters will love and cherish the soft, glimmering stockings, *at left.* Crafted from plaid taffeta fabric and even-weave fabric, these 19¼-inch stockings will take their places among your children's favorite trims for their holiday decorating.

Use scraps of 14-count Aida cloth to stitch the fringed plaid cuff and the sweet heart motif that personalizes these stockings, making them treasured keepsakes.

Crisp white snowflake designs set off the 14x14-inch pillows, *above.* These dazzling pillows will enchant anyone on your gift list or add sparkle to any cozy corner in your home.

To show them off at their best, stitch any one of the two designs with white pearl cotton on dark colored even-weave cloth. Then dress them up with contrasting piping and lots of plaid taffeta ruffles.

## Plaid Star Tree Top

Shown on page 4.

Star is approximately 10 inches from point to point.

**MATERIALS**
14x14-inch piece of 18-count ivory-white Aida cloth
DMC embroidery floss: 2 skeins *each* of green (No. 699) and red (No. 321)
DMC pearl cotton, Size 3: 1 skein of red (No. 321)
Two 11x11-inch pieces of muslin
Polyester fleece for interfacing
5-inch strip of 1-inch elastic
1 yard of ⅝-inch red ribbon

**INSTRUCTIONS**
Before beginning, see the general information on pages 78 and 79 for special cross-stitch tips and techniques, and for materials necessary for working counted cross-stitch projects.

STITCHING THE STAR: Referring to the chart, *far right,* locate the center of the design and the center of the Aida cloth; begin stitching there. Use two strands of floss to work the cross-stitches over one thread of the cloth.

Complete the stitching on this chart; then refer to the chart, *near right,* to complete the remaining two points. *Note:* The shaded portion on this chart is for placement only and to designate stitches already worked. Do not work the shaded areas.

When all the stitching is complete, press and machine-stitch around the star 1 inch beyond the cross-stitching. Then cut out the star ¼ inch beyond the machine stitching.

QUILTING THE STITCHERY: Layer, then baste together one square of the muslin, the fleece, and the stitchery, right side up. Machine- or hand-quilt along the dividing lines of the plaid patterns and around the outline of the star. Trim the edges of the fleece and muslin to within ¼ inch of the outline quilting.

ASSEMBLY: From the remaining piece of muslin, cut a matching star shape for the backing. Turn under ¼ inch on both sides of the short edges of the elastic and sew it to the muslin in the upper half of the star center. With right sides facing and using ½-inch seam allowance, sew backing and stitchery together, and leave an opening for turning. Clip corners, turn, and press. Sew the opening closed.

Refer to the instructions for the Plaid Ornaments on page 15 for making the braided cording. Use 6 yards of pearl cotton to make the cording. Couch the cording atop the outline seam edges. Tie ribbon into bow and tack to center of star. Slip elastic over top branch of tree to hang.

## Plaid Tree Ornaments

Shown on pages 4–5.

The finished ornaments measure 3x3 inches.

**MATERIALS**
7x7-inch piece of 18-count ivory Aida cloth for 1 ornament
DMC floss in the following amounts and colors to work all six ornaments: 4 skeins of green (No. 699); 3 skeins of red (No. 321)
Scraps of dark red (No. 498), blue (No. 824), brown (No. 801), orange (No. 721), gray (No. 414), black (No. 310) and white to work the motifs
Polyester fiberfill
DMC pearl cotton, Size 5, 3 yards of red (No. 321) or green (No. 699) for 1 ornament

**INSTRUCTIONS**
Before beginning, see the general information on pages 78 and 79 for special cross-stitch tips and techniques, and for materials for working cross-stitch projects.

CROSS-STITCHING THE ORNAMENTS: Refer to the chart on page 14 and select *one* of the seven plaid patterns; pattern 1b is a

reverse color pattern of 1a; 2b is a reverse of 2a; and 3b is a reverse color of 3a. Each ornament is stitched over 75 threads square.

Begin stitching 1½ inches from the bottom and the left side edges of the cloth at the red symbol on the left side of chart. Work the cross-stitches over one thread of the cloth using two strands of floss. Work the entire piece in the plaid selected. Stitch the rows between A–B for each plaid and repeat that pattern until 26 rows (threads) from the bottom are worked. Then, following the plaid *continued*

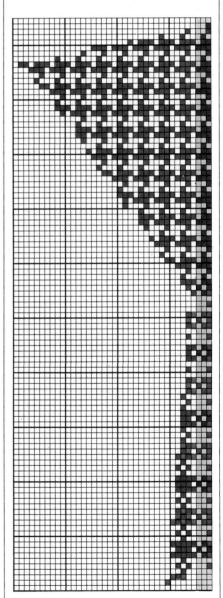

**Star Tree Top**

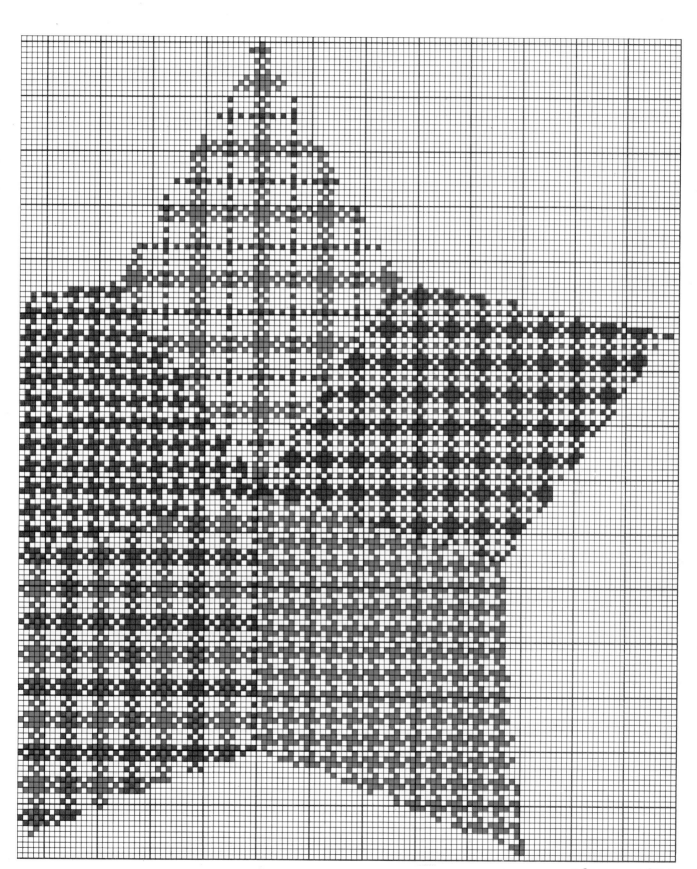

**1 Square = 1 Stitch**

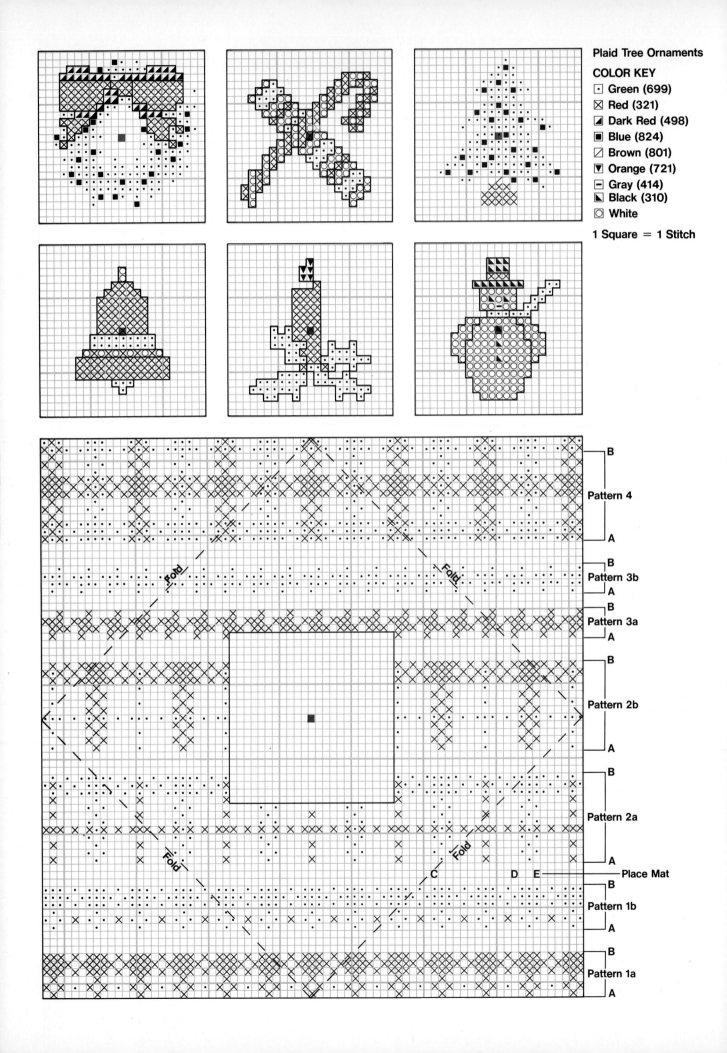

Plaid Tree Ornaments

COLOR KEY
- ⊡ Green (699)
- ⊠ Red (321)
- ◪ Dark Red (498)
- ■ Blue (824)
- ▨ Brown (801)
- ▼ Orange (721)
- ⊟ Gray (414)
- ◣ Black (310)
- ○ White

1 Square = 1 Stitch

Pattern 4
- B
- A

Pattern 3b
- B
- A

Pattern 3a
- B
- A

Pattern 2b
- B
- A

Pattern 2a
- B
- A

Place Mat

Pattern 1b
- B
- A

Pattern 1a
- B
- A

Fold

C    D  E

pattern, work the sides separately across 26 threads on *both* of the outside edges for 23 rows. (The center 23x23 threads are not stitched in the plaid.)

Stitch the top 26 rows of the plaid across the 75 threads.

Backstitch around the outside edge of the 23x23-thread square using color of your choice.

Select a motif for the center square from the top of chart, *opposite*. Locate center of motif (the red symbol) and center of the fabric; begin stitching there.

Use a single strand of floss to work the backstitching on the motifs as follows: Use gray on snowman and candy motifs; use green for bell; use brown for candle and wreath. Press the stitched piece and machine-sew around the plaid stitching; trim edges to ⅜ inch beyond the stitching.

ASSEMBLY: Fold back corner edges along fold lines, turning ⅜ inch under, and whipstitch corners together (there will be four triangles that fit together); leave edge that points to bottom of ornament unstitched; stuff lightly.

CORD AND TASSEL: Measure 3 yards of pearl cotton; cut. Fold length in half and then in half again. Fasten one end of length to nail and twist the thread until it is *tight*. Place finger in center of twisted length and, keeping the yarn tight, place the ends together. Remove finger and allow thread to twist into braid. Make knot at end. Couch the cording to the folded edges of ornament, inserting tails into the unstitched edge at back of ornament.

To make the tassel, wrap the pearl cotton 20 times around a 3x3-inch piece of cardboard. Insert a 5-inch length of pearl cotton under the wrapped thread and slip the wrapped thread from the cardboard. Knot the strand to make a bundle (the top of the tassel). Wrap another piece of pearl cotton several times around the bundle ½ inch from the top; knot. Insert tassel top ends into the opening; whipstitch edge closed. Cut bottom of tassel. Sew hanger to top of ornament.

## Plaid Place Mats And Napkins

Shown on pages 6–7.

Finished mat is 12x19 inches.

### MATERIALS
**For the place mats**
For each mat, one piece of ivory-white hardanger measuring 16x21 inches.
DMC embroidery floss in the following amounts and colors: 1 skein *each* of red (No. 321) and green (No. 699)
**For the napkins**
Purchased ivory napkins
DMC embroidery floss in colors cited for the motifs of the tree ornaments on page 12
5x5-inch piece of 10-count waste canvas for one napkin

### INSTRUCTIONS
STITCHING THE MATS: Referring to chart, *opposite*, select plaid pattern of your choice (we used pattern 1a for the horizontal-stripe mat and pattern 2a for the vertical pattern). Use two strands of floss to work the cross-stitches over two threads of the fabric.

To work the mat with the vertical stripe (pattern 2a), begin stitching 3½ inches from the left edge of the fabric and 2 inches from the bottom edge. Begin at C and work *across* to D; then work from C to E to complete first row of stitching. Follow this sequence to work *horizontally* and at the same time, repeat the pattern between A and B for 12 inches.

To work the mat with the horizontal stripe (1a), begin stitching the bottom band 2 inches from the left edge and 2½ inches from the bottom edge of the cloth. Work the stitches across the row until 2 inches remain unworked. Work the pattern between A and B 3 times; then work 3 more rows from A. To work the top band, begin stitching 4½ inches from the top edge of the cloth and 2 inches from the left side edge. Follow instructions for the bottom band for working from the chart.

FINISHING: To finish the mat with the vertical stripe, machine-sew a straight line 2 inches in from *both* the right and left side edges. Then pull away the vertical threads to fringe; trim the fringe to measure 1 inch. Trim the top and bottom edges to ¾ inch from stitching and hem.

To finish the mat with the horizontal bands, make fringed edges following directions, *above*. Trim top and bottom edges to 1¼ inches from stitching and hem.

**For the napkins**
Center and baste the waste canvas to one corner edge of the napkin. Referring to chart, *opposite*, select motif of your choice. Beginning in center of canvas, work each cross-stitch over 1 square of the canvas using four threads of floss.

When all stitching is complete, remove the basting threads and carefully cut away the unworked waste canvas (allow ½ inch of canvas around the motif). Dampen the remaining canvas with water and pull out the horizontal threads one at a time and then repeat for the vertical threads.

## Plaid Throw And Pillows

Shown on pages 8–9.

Finished size of throw is 54x63 inches; pillows are 14x14 inches.

### MATERIALS
**For the throw**
1⅔ yards of 54-inch-wide plaid wool fabric
½ yard of 54-inch-wide red wool fabric
3-ply Paternayan yarns in the following amounts and colors: 20 strands of green (No. 611), 2 strands of brown (No. 412), and 8 strands of blue (No. 341)
6x54-inch piece of 10-count waste canvas
½ yard of narrow cotton cording
*continued*

**For one pillow**

½ yard of 54-inch-wide plaid wool fabric

Scraps of red and green wool fabrics

8x8-inch piece of off-white wool

6x6-inch piece of 10-count waste canvas

3-ply Paternayan yarn in the following amounts and colors: *For the snowman,* 1 strand of white, scraps of black, red, and green. *For the candle,* 1 strand of red and green, and scraps of yellow. *For the wreath,* 2 strands of green, 1 strand of blue and red, scraps of rose and brown

1⅔ yards of narrow cotton cording

Polyester fiberfill

## INSTRUCTIONS

*Note:* All sewing allows for ½-inch seam allowances.

THROW: Cut one 1½-inch-wide strip from the short side of the plaid fabric; set aside.

From the red fabric, cut a strip measuring 12x54 inches. Center and baste the waste canvas along *one* long side of the right side of the red fabric just inside the seam allowance. Fold the strip in half with short edges matching to locate the center of the strip; mark with pin.

Referring to the tree motif, page 14, begin cross-stitching at the center stitch of the bottom row of the tree trunk ½ inch from the waste canvas edge. Work each cross-stitch over two squares of the waste canvas using one ply of the yarn.

Allowing 10 squares of waste canvas between each tree motif, work five trees to the right and five trees to the left of the center one. *Note:* The 10 squares are between the two outermost limbs of the trees.

When all the cross-stitching is complete, remove the basting threads and carefully cut away the unworked waste canvas (allow ½ inch of canvas around the trees). To remove the remaining canvas, dampen it with water and pull away the horizontal threads one at a time and then pull away the vertical threads.

With right sides facing, fold the red strip in half, *lengthwise,* and machine-sew the two short edges (do not sew into the seam allowance along the raw edges); turn and press. Set strip aside.

Cover the cording with the 1½-inch-wide strip of plaid fabric. With right sides together, sew the cording along one short edge of the plaid fabric (for the top of throw).

Press and turn under the remaining three sides of the plaid fabric ¼ inch toward the *right side* of the throw. Then press and turn the edges ⅜ inch toward the right side.

From the remaining piece of red fabric cut four strips, *each* 1x54 inches. Sew and piece two strips to measure the length of the throw. Fold the red strips in half, *lengthwise,* and place the raw edges under the folded edges of the three sides of the plaid throw; baste in place. Topstitch along the folded plaid edge through all the thicknesses.

With right sides facing, sew the embroidered edge of the red band to the right side of the plaid fabric. Turn under the seam allowance on the back side of the red band and hand-sew it in place atop the seam line on the reverse side of the throw.

PILLOWS: Center, then baste the waste canvas to the 8-inch square of off-white fabric. Using any one of the motifs of your choice on page 14, locate the center of the design and the center of the canvas; begin stitching there. With one ply of yarn, work cross-stitches over two squares of the waste canvas. When stitching is complete, remove canvas as directed for throw, *above.* Keeping the design centered, cut square to measure 7x7 inches; set aside.

CANDLE PILLOW: Cut out four 3x7-inch strips from the red fabric. Repeat for green fabric. Cut out four 5x5-inch blocks from the plaid fabric.

Using the photo on page 8 as a guide, piece all the strips and squares and sew to center block log-cabin style. Press all seams.

FINISHING: Cut 1½-inch-wide bias strips from red fabric and piece to make 60-inch strip. Using zipper foot, cover cotton cording with bias strip to make piping. With right sides facing, sew piping along seam allowance to pillow top, finishing ends.

Cut backing from plaid fabric to measure 15x15 inches. With right sides facing, sew top to back, leaving an opening for turning. Clip corners, turn, and stuff.

WREATH PILLOW: Work cross-stitching on center block following instructions for Pillows, *left.*

Cut twelve 3x3-inch squares from red fabric. Repeat for green fabric. Cut four 5x5-inch squares from plaid fabric.

Using the photo on page 8 as a guide, piece three red and three green squares together to make one band. Make three more bands. Sew bands and squares to center block, log-cabin style, to complete pillow top.

Complete pillow following Finishing instructions, *above,* using red fabric for piping.

SNOWMAN PILLOW: Work the stitching on the center block following instructions for Pillows, *left.*

Cut eight 3x3-inch squares from red fabric. Repeat for green fabric. Cut four 5x7-inch strips from plaid fabric. Referring to photo on page 9 as a guide, piece two red and two green squares to make one corner block. Make three more corner blocks.

Sew one plaid strip to center block, right sides facing. Assemble pieced blocks to plaid strips and sew to center block log-cabin style to complete pillow top.

Complete pillow following Finishing instructions, *above.*

# Plaid Stockings

Shown on page 10.

Stockings are 19¼ inches tall.

**MATERIALS**
**For one stocking**
6x21-inch strip of 14-count cream Aida cloth
DMC embroidery floss: 1 skein *each* of red (No. 321) and green (No. 699)
1 yard of 44-inch-wide plaid taffeta
2 pieces of 19x22-inch polyester fleece
2 yards of narrow cotton cording
1⅝ yards of red or green ribbon

**INSTRUCTIONS**
CUFF: Cut 6x18-inch strip of Aida cloth; set small piece aside. Referring to the chart, *bottom, far right*, begin cross-stitching 4 inches from the top of the cloth and 1 inch from the left-side edge. Use two strands of floss to work the cross-stitches over 1 thread of the cloth. Read the chart from left to right, beginning at A and working to B; then repeat the chart from A to B. Continue across the row in this manner until 1 inch remains unworked. Work the remaining 26 rows of cross-stitch plaid following the sequence as directed, *above*.

When all stitching is complete, machine-sew *horizontally* one stitch beyond the *first* row of stitching. Cut away excess cloth along bottom edge, leaving 1 inch to fringe. Pull away the horizontal threads to make fringe.

Cut away excess cloth above the top stitching edge, leaving 1 inch. With right sides facing, sew the two short sides together; set cuff aside.

STOCKING: Enlarge stocking shape, *top right*, onto graph paper. Add ½-inch seam allowance. Cut four stocking shapes from plaid taffeta and two from the polyester fleece. Set two taffeta shapes aside for the lining. Baste the fleece to the *wrong* side of the shapes for front and back of

stocking. Cover the cording with bias-cut strips of taffeta to make piping. Sew piping to right side of one stocking piece; do not sew piping along top edge or in seam allowances at top of stocking.

With the right sides facing, sew stocking front to stocking back, leaving top edge free; clip curves. Turn stocking right side out.

Sew cuff, then piping, to top of stocking.

With right sides together, sew two lining pieces together; trim seam edges. Turn back and press seam allowance at top edge. Slip lining into stocking and hand-sew lining in place, tucking in cuff and piping edges.

HEART: Using red or green floss, center and cross-stitch your child's name onto the remaining piece of Aida cloth. It is best to chart the name onto graph paper before beginning your stitching. Use block-style letters, referring to the Country Angel pinafore letters on page 53 for a guide.

Using chart, *below*, center the heart motif 2 stitches from the bottom line of the name and work cross-stitches.

Draw a heart shape that accommodates the stitching and cut shape from the stitched piece and the taffeta for backing. Sew piping to stitched piece. With right sides facing, sew front to back; clip curves, turn, and press. Tie 1½ yards of ribbon into bow and sew to side edge of stocking. Tack heart shape to one end of ribbon ties. Fold and tack the remaining 4½-inch strip of ribbon to side edge for hanger.

**Plaid Stocking**

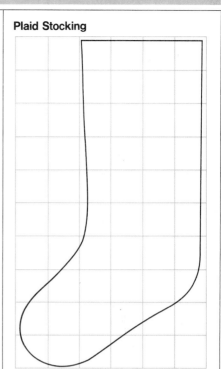

1 Square = 2 Inches

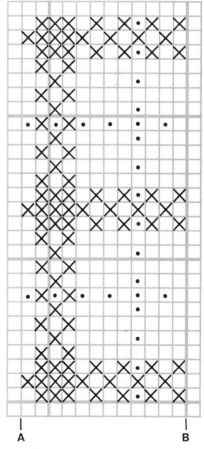

A                                    B

**Plaid Stocking Cuff**
**COLOR KEY**
☒ Green (699)
⊡ Red (321)
1 Square = 1 Stitch

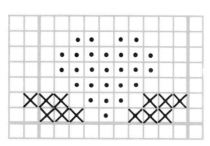

**Plaid Stocking Heart**
**1 Square = 1 Stitch**

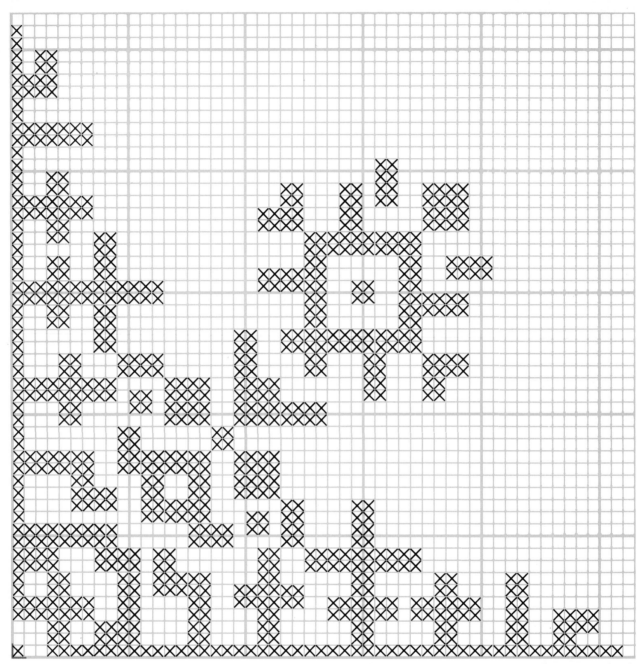

**Snowflake Pillows**

1 Square = 1 Stitch

# Snowflake Pillows

Shown on page 11.

Pillows are 14x14 inches, excluding ruffles.

**MATERIALS**
**For one pillow**

18x18-inch piece of 18-count blue or green Davosa cloth
DMC No. 8 pearl cotton (95-yard ball): 1 ball of white
⅞ yard of 44-inch-wide plaid taffeta for backing and ruffles
1⅔ yards of narrow cotton cording; scraps of red or green cotton fabric to cover cording
Polyester fiberfill
Graph paper

**INSTRUCTIONS**

CROSS-STITCHING THE PILLOWS: Refer to photo, page 11, and select snowflake design of your choice. The chart for the pillow on the top right in the photo is *above;* the pillow on the bottom left is on page 19. Both charts show quadrants of the designs. Transfer the complete design onto graph paper, flopping the design to make mirror images in the remaining three quadrants. Begin stitching the design in the

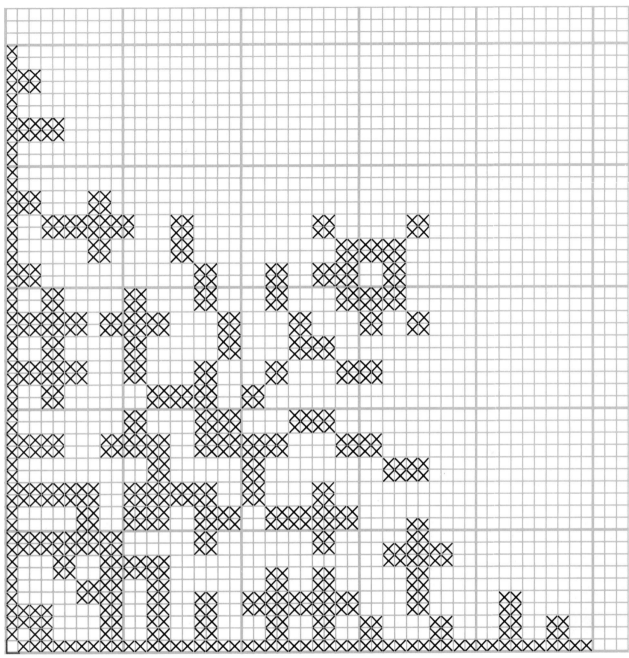

**Snowflake Pillows**

1 Square = 1 Stitch

center of the fabric at the center of the design. Use one strand of pearl cotton to work the cross-stitches over two threads of the fabric.

When stitching is complete, center the design and cut the fabric to measure 15x15 inches.

FINISHING: All sewing allows for ½-inch seam allowances.

Cover cording with red or green cotton to make piping and sew to pillow top.

For the ruffle, cut two 6x44-inch strips from the taffeta; sew short ends together, right sides facing. With wrong sides together, fold tube in half, raw edges even. Gather ruffle to fit pillow. Sew ruffle to pillow top.

Cut 15x15-inch backing from plaid fabric. With right sides together, sew backing to top, leaving an opening for turning. Clip curves, turn, and stuff. Sew opening closed.

# EVERYWHERE,
## EVERYWHERE
# CHRISTMAS TONIGHT

♦♦♦

Memories of holidays long ago hold a special place in our hearts. To help you recall those earlier times, here is a treasure of beautifully old-fashioned designs—samplers, ornaments and trims, and lovely home accents—all fashioned with a mood that re-creates a bygone era.

The nighttime village scene, *opposite,* captures the essence of a quiet Christmas eve. This 9¼x10¼-inch stitchery, with its snow-laden evergreens, soft lights reflecting from the village church and houses, and twinkling stars glittering in the sky, is full of enchanting magic to bring the spirit of Christmas into your heart and home.

Worked on 18-count even-weave fabric, using embroidery floss and metallic threads, this unique stitchery is matted with its seasonal message. Follow the instructions provided for making the mat, or take your stitchery to a professional framer and calligrapher for guaranteed results.

Instructions for the projects in this chapter begin on page 28.

# CHRISTMAS TONIGHT

This Christmas, make a special gift for a little one by stitching the 9½x9½-inch pillow, *below,* adapted from the sampler design, *at right.* The joy it will bring will be well worth your time and efforts.

This glimpse of Christmas morning is stitched on 18-count even-weave fabric, piped with contrasting bias fabric, and framed with lots of ruffles.

The 10⅜x12-inch sampler, *at right,* with its magical silhouettes, tells an old-fashioned Christmas story. Select ivory 14-count Aida cloth and subtle red embroidery floss to stitch this bygone-days' treasure.

Use one of the designs in the sampler to stitch the precious hearth stool, *at right.* We used ivory threads on a red 18-count even-weave fabric, but you can easily select the colors of your choice to fit your holiday or year-round decorating scheme.

# CHRISTMAS TONIGHT

S oft pastel snowflake ornaments set the mood for this romantic old-fashioned Christmas as they cascade over the tree, *at left*. More designs, *below,* adorn captivating packages.

All five of these trims easily are stitched onto perforated paper using embroidery floss. Then, when the stitching is complete, carefully cut away the unstitched paper. To finish the medallion ornament, *below,* add pregathered lace and a ribbon bow for a soft, delicate touch.

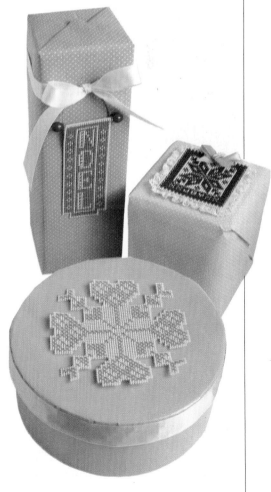

# CHRISTMAS TONIGHT

A sleigh loaded with packages and happy folks, the sound of jingling bells, and the crisp whites of December's first snowfall—these are the recollections of an old-fashioned Christmas. The snow-sparkling sampler, *opposite,* captures the delightful spirit and feeling of Christmases past.

A lovely holiday keepsake, this 18x21-inch sampler is stitched onto 18-count even-weave fabric, using 3-ply woolen yarns.

You can frame the stitchery as shown here, or adapt it into an album cover to keep holiday photos for years to come. Whether you craft this sampler for a friend or a family member, it's a gift with a warm, personal touch.

# CHRISTMAS TONIGHT

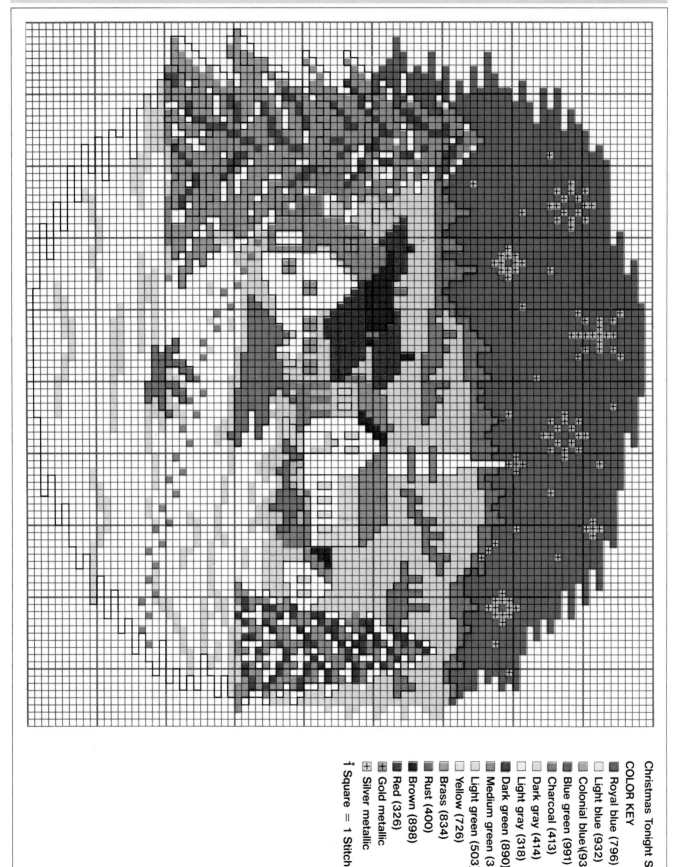

**Christmas Tonight Sampler**

**COLOR KEY**

- ◼ Royal blue (796)
- ◻ Light blue (932)
- ◻ Colonial blue (931)
- ◼ Blue green (991)
- ◼ Charcoal (413)
- ◻ Dark gray (414)
- ◻ Light gray (318)
- ◼ Dark green (890)
- ◼ Medium green (367)
- ◼ Light green (503)
- ◻ Yellow (726)
- ◼ Brass (834)
- ◼ Rust (400)
- ◼ Brown (898)
- ◼ Red (326)
- ⊞ Gold metallic
- ⊞ Silver metallic

1 Square = 1 Stitch

E V R Y

W H -

C I S T

M A

O N I G

**Christmas Tonight Sampler
Full-size Pattern**

## Christmas Tonight Sampler

Shown on pages 20–21.

Finished size of framed stitchery is 17x17 inches.

### MATERIALS

13½x14½-inch piece of 18-count Aida cloth
DMC embroidery floss, 1 skein *each* of the following colors: royal blue (No. 796), light blue (No. 932), colonial blue (No. 931), blue-green (No. 991), charcoal (No. 413), dark gray (No. 414), light gray (No. 318), dark green (No. 890), medium green (No. 367), light green (No. 503), yellow (No. 726), brass (No. 834), rust (No. 400), brown (No. 898), and red (No. 326)
Gold and silver metallic threads
Tracing paper; calligraphy pen and ink

### INSTRUCTIONS

Before beginning, see the general information on pages 78 and 79 for special cross-stitch tips and techniques.

Referring to the chart, *opposite*, locate the center of the design and the center of the Aida cloth; begin stitching there. Use two strands of floss to work the cross-stitches over two threads of the cloth.

When all the cross-stitching is complete, work the backstitching as follows: Use charcoal to outline the village skyline, houses, and church; use blue-green to outline the blue-green shrubs; use dark green to outline the evergreen trees; use light gray to outline the snow.

When stitching is complete, press on wrong side with warm iron. Cut mat as desired for the inside opening, having outside dimensions of 15½x15½ inches. Trace the mat shape onto tracing paper and draw an arc along the top and bottom edges of the inside opening. Use the letters, *at left*, to write the greeting along the arc lines as shown on photo on page 20. Transfer lettering to the mat and complete calligraphy; frame.

**Christmas Sampler**

COLOR KEY    ☒ Red (347)

1 Square = 1 Stitch

## Christmas Sampler

Shown on page 23.

Finished size of the stitched piece is 10⅜x12 inches.

**MATERIALS**
16x18 inch piece of 14-count ivory Aida cloth
DMC embroidery floss: 10 skeins of red (No. 347); 1 skein of ivory (No. 712)

**INSTRUCTIONS**
Refer to the chart, *opposite*, and begin the cross-stitching at the upper left corner of the chart 3¾ inches from both the top and left side edges of the fabric (at the red symbol) and work the heart border all around. Use 3 strands of floss to work the stitches over 1 thread of the fabric. *Note:* The chart shows only 3 sides of the border. Rotate the chart to work the border along the bottom sides. Work the corner motif in all 4 corners.

Stitch the inside portions of the sampler. Then, backstitch the mouse's tail, the candle flames, and the "Merry Christmas." Use ivory to make long stitches for the wire of the picture above the bed, for the reins, and to work the backstitches for the house windows. Frame as desired.

## Christmas Pillow

Shown on page 22.

Finished size of pillow, excluding ruffle, is 9½x9½ inches.

**MATERIALS**
13½x13½ piece of red 18-count Kappie cloth
DMC embroidery floss: 2 skeins of ivory (No. 712)
½ yard of 44-inch-wide heather green wool for ruffle and backing
2⅓ yards of red double-fold tape
1¼ yards of narrow cotton cording; scrap of contrasting fabric to cover cording
Polyester fiberfill

**INSTRUCTIONS**
Before beginning, see the general information on pages 78 and 79 for special cross-stitch tips and techniques, and for materials necessary for working counted cross-stitch projects.

CROSS-STITCHING THE DESIGN: Locate the center of the design (the red symbol) in the lower right corner of the chart, *opposite*, and the center of the Kappie cloth; begin stitching there. Use 4 strands of floss to work the cross-stitches over 2 threads of the cloth. Work the flames of the candles with backstitches.

*Note:* The right and bottom borders on the pillow are mirror images of the left and top borders as shown on the chart. Work the top border across until 14 diamond motifs are completed; then work the right border until 14 motifs are completed. Work the remaining 2 sides to match.

When all stitching is complete, press on wrong side. Trim the piece to measure 10½x10½ inches, keeping the design centered.

PILLOW ASSEMBLY: Cover the cording with the contrasting fabric to make piping. Sew the piping along the ½-inch seam allowance of the stitched piece, right sides facing.

From green wool, cut backing to match the stitched piece and 2 strips *each* measuring 2¾x44 inches. Sew strips of wool together to make a tube, right sides facing; press and zigzag seams.

Baste, then topstitch, the double-fold tape to 1 long edge of the assembled strips. Gather along the raw edges to fit the pillow top and sew in place atop piping seam. With right sides together, sew front to back, leaving opening for turning. Clip corners, turn, press, and stuff. Sew opening closed.

## Hearth Stool

Shown on page 23.

Finished size of stitched piece is 5⅝x6 inches.

### MATERIALS

10x10-inch piece of red Kappie cloth
DMC embroidery floss: 2 skeins of ivory (No. 712)
Graph paper
Hearth stool with a 6⅜x6⅜-inch inset (available at crafts shops or by writing to Plain n' Fancy, Inc. P. O. Box 756, Jensen Beach, FL 33457)

### INSTRUCTIONS

Before beginning, see the general information on pages 78 and 79 for special cross-stitch tips and techniques, and for materials necessary for working counted cross-stitch projects.

CROSS-STITCHING THE DESIGN: Referring to the chart, *below,* transfer the design to graph paper. Flop the design once to make a mirror image.

Locate the center of your chart (red symbol), and the center of the Kappie cloth; begin stitching there. Use 4 strands of floss to work the cross-stitches over 2 threads of the cloth. When all stitching is complete, press on the wrong side.

ASSEMBLING: Remove the insert on the top of the stool. Center and lay the insert *atop* the stitchery, wrong side up. Fold the fabric to the back, trimming away the excess cloth, and tape in place. *Note:* Do not cover the holes on the insert for the mounting screws. Mount the insert to the stool following the manufacturer's directions.

## Medallion Ornament

Shown on page 25.

Ornament is 2½x2¾ inches.

### MATERIALS

3½x4-inch piece of ecru or white perforated paper for 1 ornament (see Snowflake Ornaments, page 32, for source for paper)
DMC embroidery floss in color of your choice
⅓ yard of ecru pregathered cotton lace
6 inches of ¼-inch-wide satin ribbon; crafts glue

### INSTRUCTIONS

Before beginning, see the general information on pages 78 and 79 for special cross-stitch tips and techniques for working counted cross-stitch projects.

Refer to the medallion motif in the lower left corner of the Christmas Sampler, page 30. Locate the center of the design and the center of the paper; begin stitching there. Use 2 strands of floss to work cross-stitches over 1 square of the paper. When all the stitching is complete, carefully cut around the design one row of squares beyond the stitching.

Glue the lace to the wrong side of the stitched piece. Tie ribbon into bow; glue to center top of ornament. Add hanger as desired.

**Snowflake Ornaments**

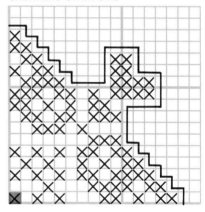

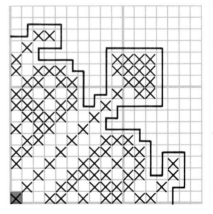

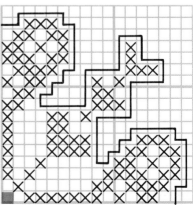

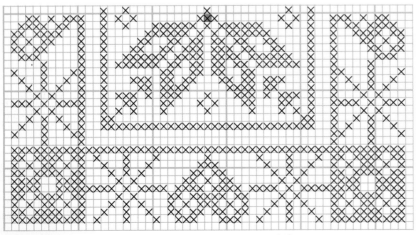

**Hearth Stool**     1 Square = 1 Stitch

1 Square = 1 Stitch

# Snowflake Ornaments

Shown on pages 24–25.

Ornaments are approximately 4½ inches in diameter.

## MATERIALS
9x12-inch sheet of ecru or white perforated paper to make 3 ornaments or 5x5-inch piece of perforated paper for 1 ornament (available at crafts stores or by writing to Astor Place, Ltd., 239 Main Avenue, Stirling, NJ 07980)
DMC embroidery floss in the colors of your choice
Graph paper

## INSTRUCTIONS
Before beginning, see the general information on pages 78 and 79 for special cross-stitch tips and techniques.

Referring to charts on page 32, *far right*, select snowflake design of your choice and transfer to graph paper. Chart mirror images in the remaining 3 quadrants. Locate the center of your chart (red symbol) and the center of the perforated paper; begin stitching there. Use 4 strands of floss to work the cross-stitches over 2 squares of the paper. When all cross-stitching is complete, carefully cut around the design one row of squares beyond the stitching. *Note:* Solid line on chart indicates the cutting line.

# Noel Ornament

Shown on page 25.

Ornament is 1⅝x4⅛ inches.

## MATERIALS
3x5-inch piece of white or ecru perforated paper (see Snowflake Ornaments, *above,* for source) for 1 ornament
DMC embroidery floss in colors of your choice
Toothpick; 2 wooden beads
10-inch strand of gold braid
Crafts glue

## INSTRUCTIONS
Referring to chart, *below,* locate the center of the design (red X) and the center of the paper; begin stitching there. Use 2 strands of floss to work the cross-stitches over 1 square of the paper. When all cross-stitching is complete, carefully cut around the design one row of squares beyond the stitching.

Center and glue toothpick to wrong side of ornament top. Glue wooden beads to ends of toothpick; trim ends. Tie gold braid to each side between ornament and beads; trim ends.

**Noel Ornament**

**1 Square = 1 Stitch**

# Sleigh-Ride Sampler

Shown on pages 26–27.

Unframed stitchery is approximately 18x21 inches.

## MATERIALS
24x29-inch piece of 18-count white Davosa
Paternayan 3-ply Persian yarn in the following amounts and colors: 10 strands *each* of dark blue (No. 501) and light blue (No. 504); 7 strands *each* of dark green (No. 661) and white (No. 260); 6 strands *each* of gold (No. 731), golden brown (No. 412), and taupe (No. 462); 5 strands of dark brown (No. 410); 4 strands *each* of dark gray (No. 221), medium gray (No. 211), and light gray (No. 212); 3 strands of bright blue (No. 551); 1 strand *each* of yellow (No. 711) and flesh (No. 406)
DMC embroidery floss, scraps of dark gray (No. 844), medium gray (No. 317), and dark brown (No. 610) for backstitching
Graph paper

## INSTRUCTIONS
Referring to the chart on pages 34 and 35, chart your name, family names, date, or any other message onto graph paper to fill in the open area at the bottom of the sampler. Make sure message fits within the space on the chart before you begin your stitching.

Locate the center of the design (the red symbol on page 34), and the center of the fabric; begin stitching there. Work all cross-stitches with 1 strand of yarn over two threads of the fabric.

Work backstitching with 3 strands of floss as follows: Use medium gray to outline the roof, trees, and rabbits; dark gray to work the reins; and dark brown to outline the elks.

When all stitching is complete, press on wrong side and frame.

# CHRISTMAS TONIGHT

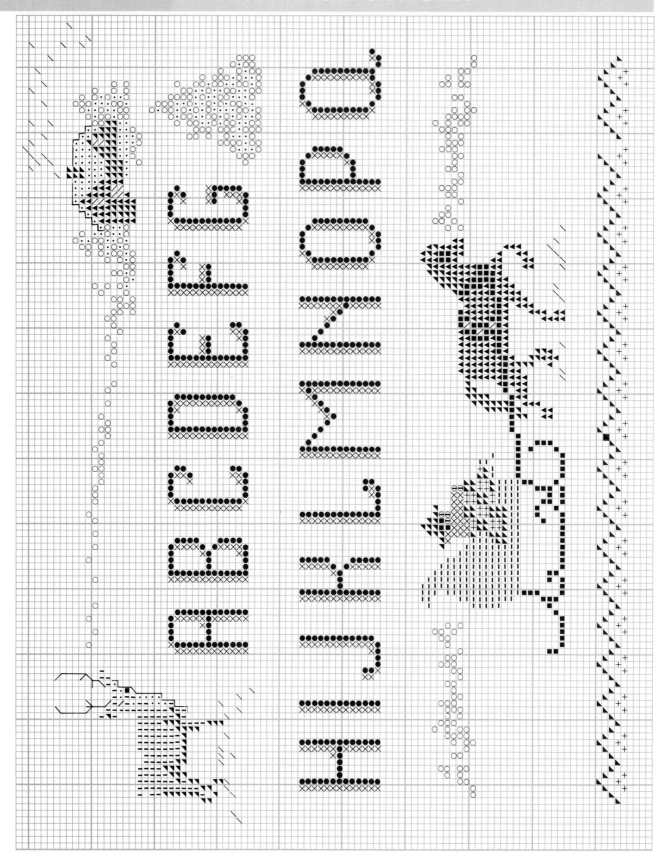

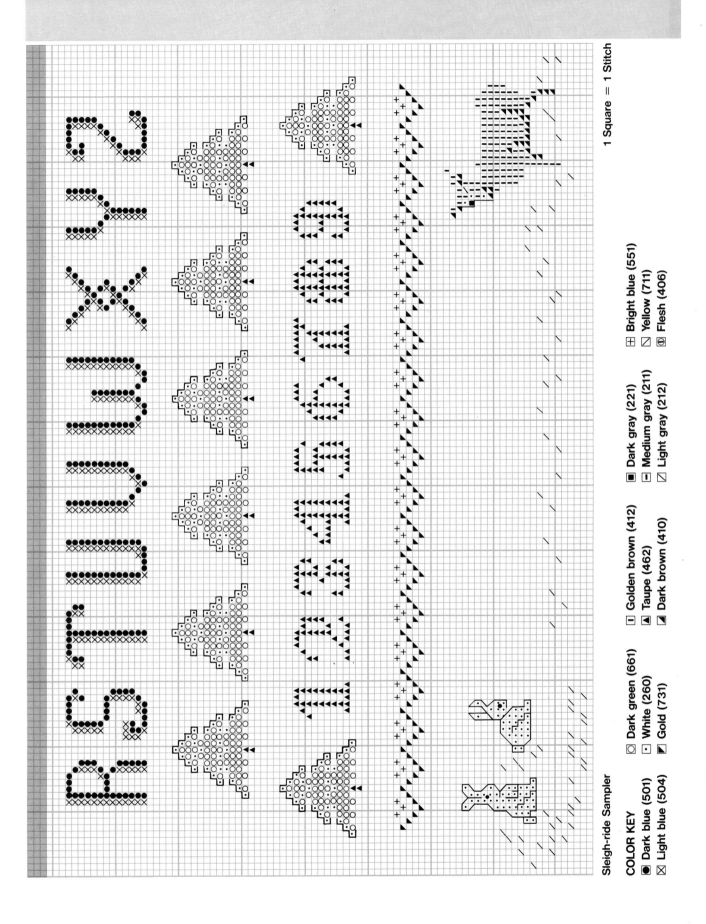

1 Square = 1 Stitch

**Sleigh-ride Sampler**

**COLOR KEY**
◉ Dark blue (501)
⊠ Light blue (504)
○ Dark green (661)
· White (260)
▮ Gold (731)
Ⅰ Golden brown (412)
▲ Taupe (462)
◢ Dark brown (410)
▪ Dark gray (221)
⊟ Medium gray (211)
⬚ Light gray (212)
⊞ Bright blue (551)
⧄ Yellow (711)
◈ Flesh (406)

*Silent night,. holy night, all is calm, all is bright. Rou*

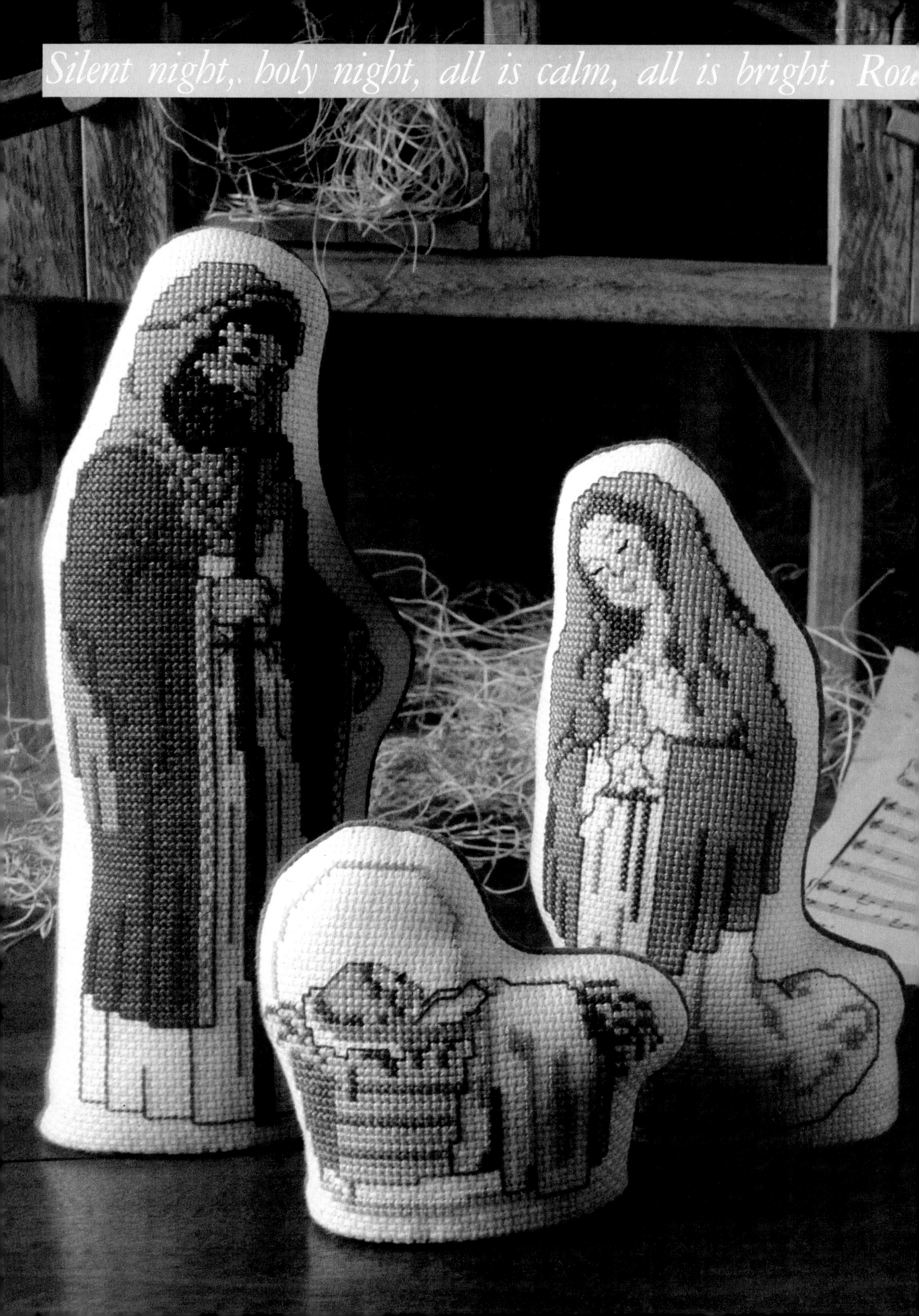

# A STITCHERY FOR
# CHRISTMAS CAROLS

❖❖❖

Bells pealing, choirs singing, children laughing—these are the wonderful sounds of Christmas. And our heritage of lovely Christmas music highlights this season and celebrates its grandeur. In this chapter, samplers, stockings, and ornamental trims are among the cross-stitch designs that honor five favorite carols.

Serene as the carol that inspired them, the three-dimensional crèche figures, *below* and *opposite*, recapture the humble scene of Christ's birth on that silent and holy night.

Stitch them onto individual pieces of Aida cloth and use touches of backstitching for outlines and facial expressions.

Each stitchery is lined with fleece for stability, weighted in each base, and backed with velveteen. How-to instructions for projects in this chapter begin on page 46.

*all the trees that are in the wood the holly bears the*

References to the combination of holly and ivy have appeared in British writings for centuries, but none is as well known as the carol sung today. Holly, with its waxy green leaves and red berries, has special significance. Ivy, with its trailing vines of new growth, suggests everlasting life. The exquisite framed stitchery and stocking, *opposite*, are beautiful interpretations of these holiday greens.

The 20x20-inch wreath motif is worked onto 11-count even-weave fabric, using embroidery floss. As an alternative to framing this design, center the stitchery on a tablecloth to create a lasting greenery centerpiece.

Or, for a less complex design that celebrates this age-old carol, you can stitch the accompanying 18-inch-tall stocking. For added elegance, pipe, back, and line the stocking with a matching shade of moiré taffeta.

The peasant angel, *opposite,* pays tribute to the trumpeting carol that heralds the birth of Christ. Her apron, with all its sampler motifs, conveys the role of the angels who celebrated Christmas Eve a long time ago.

Fashioned from muslin and calico prints, this 14½-inch-tall angel is designed for display. Beneath her ruffled skirt is a form stitched from muslin that is firmly stuffed to enable the angel to stand upright as a Christmas centerpiece. Or you can easily turn this design into a treetop ornament by simply leaving the muslin form unstuffed. Then hem the edges of the muslin and slip her ruffled skirt over the top tree branch.

Saint Nick himself and his bag of goodies are the cross-stitched subjects on the front of the stocking, *opposite.* His familiar red suit, bag, and the toys and packages on the toe of the sock are stitched with floss. The trim on his suit is stitched with angora yarn to create a furry texture. Add purchased appliqués and buttons in the shapes of toy animals and other gifts to stuff his bag.

A jingle bell on Santa's hat, a braided cord for his bag, and real ribbon bows on the packages add a lively dimension.

Just the face from the stocking, *opposite,* is used for Santa's treat bag, *above.* This stitchery is attached to the front of a fabric bag, modeled after a brown paper lunch sack. Change the message to make a personalized greeting card for a child. Or omit the message and stitch only Santa's face to make a charming ornament.

Few carols inspire as much rollicking imagery as "The Twelve Days of Christmas." The lyrics of this favorite carol also inspired the masterful 16¾x22-inch framed stitchery, *opposite.* The stitched verses are placed on hardanger so that the entire song forms the silhouette of a Christmas tree.

Use embroidery floss to backstitch the letters and numerals in the lyrics. Then stitch a cluster of beads in various colors to fill in each letter "O" to simulate Christmas tree ornaments.

Metallic gold pear motifs flank the tree, and a regal partridge perches atop its branches. Adapt the individual pear and corner motifs to trim a set of holiday place mats, or stitch just the partridge to create a tree ornament.

## Christmas Crèche

Shown on pages 36–37.

The figures vary in sizes; Joseph is 8¾ inches tall.

### MATERIALS

12x44-inch piece of white 14-count Aida cloth

DMC embroidery floss in the following amounts and colors: 1 skein *each* of dark blue (No. 797), light blue (No. 809), rust brown (No. 434), light rust (No. 3064), brown (No. 839), red brown (No. 918), earth brown (No. 300), golden yellow (No. 742), yellow (No. 726), flesh (No. 951), peach (No. 758), pink (No. 962), black (No. 310), light green (No. 993), dark green (No. 991), fawn brown (No. 632), dark gray (No. 414), light gray (No. 3072), and tan (No. 841)

½ yard of 44-inch-wide gray cotton velveteen fabric for backing

¼ yard of 45-inch-wide polyester fleece

Scraps of fusible webbing

Polyester fiberfill

Graph paper

Water-erasable pen

Scraps of muslin and sand

Tracing paper

Lightweight cardboard

### INSTRUCTIONS

Specific instructions for each figure are given separately, but for all figures the following directions apply: Locate the center of *each* appropriate chart and center of the fabric; begin stitching there. Use 2 strands of floss to work the cross-stitches and the backstitches over 1 thread of the Aida cloth.

JOSEPH: Cut one 7x12-inch piece of Aida cloth. Work all cross-stitching, referring to chart on page 47. Work backstitches as follows: Use dark green to outline head piece; use rust brown to outline hands, face, and features; use red-brown to outline cloak; fawn brown to outline dress; and earth brown to outline staff. Satin-stitch eyes with black.

MARY: Cut one 8x10-inch piece of Aida cloth. Work all the cross-stitching, referring to chart on page 48. Work the back-stitches as follows: Use dark blue to outline head piece; rust brown to outline dress; light rust to outline hands, face, and features, and black to outline eyes. Satin-stitch mouth with pink.

INFANT: Cut one piece of Aida cloth to measure 7x7 inches. Work all the cross-stitching, referring to the chart on page 48. Work the backstitches as follows: Use dark blue to outline the coverlet and clothing; rust brown to outline infant's hair; light rust to outline face; and dark gray to outline the bottom of the manger. Work one half-cross with black to make the eyelash.

DONKEY: Cut one 7x8½-inch piece of Aida cloth. Work all the cross-stitching, referring to the chart on page 47. Work the backstitches with brown.

SHEEP: Cut one 6x6-inch piece of cloth for standing sheep; cut second piece 5½x6 inches for the kneeling sheep. Referring to the chart on page 46, stitch the standing sheep. Work the backstitches covering the body with light rust; work the backstitches outlining the sheep with brown.

Chart the kneeling sheep onto graph paper, making a mirror image of the standing sheep but eliminating the legs. Work the stitching following the directions for the standing sheep.

ASSEMBLY: Lay tracing paper atop the stitched pieces and trace around shapes ¾ inch beyond the design, keeping the curves smooth and making a straight line along the bottom edges to ensure that the figure stands flat. Cut out shapes.

Lay the traced shapes atop the figures and, using the water-erasable pen, draw around each of the stitcheries. Back each figure with fleece and machine-sew atop the drawn lines through both thicknesses. Machine zig-zag across bottom of figures just outside the stitching line. Cut out shapes.

Cut backing pieces from velveteen to match the front side. Machine-stitch along bottom edge of each figure ¼ inch from fabric edge. With right sides together and using ¼-inch seam allowances, sew fronts and backs together leaving bottom edge open; clip curves, turn, and press. Turn bottom seam allowance inward and baste; lightly stuff upper half of figure.

Stand figures atop tracing paper and trace around bottoms to make base patterns. Then cut base shapes from cardboard, cutting pieces ⅛ inch smaller all around than the drawn patterns. From fusible webbing, cut pieces to match the cardboard shapes and fuse the cardboard to the wrong side of the backing fabric. From the velveteen fabric, cut the base pieces ½ inch beyond the cardboard edges. Sew gathering threads atop the velveteen with ¼-inch seams around the cardboard. Pull the gathering threads tight and tie.

Make small muslin bags and fill with sand; slip bags into bases of figures. Add stuffing and whip-stitch bases to figures.

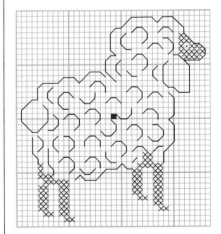

**Sheep**

**COLOR KEY**

⊠ Black (310)

⊡ Blue (809)

**1 Square = 1 Stitch**

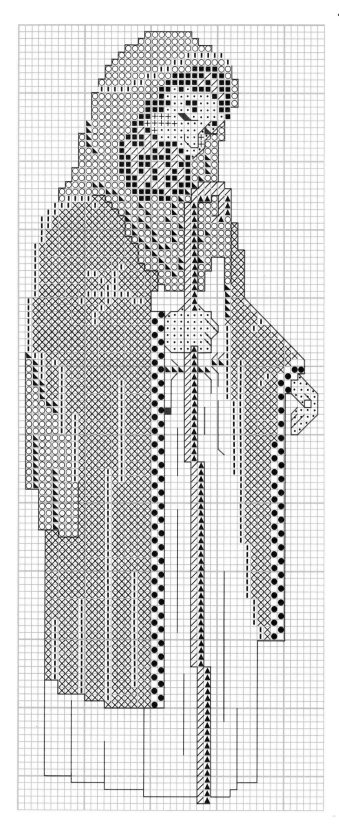

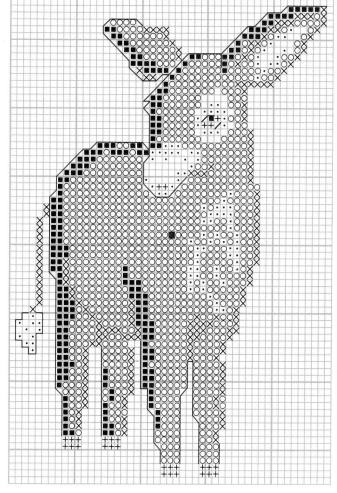

**Joseph**

**COLOR KEY**

⊘ Light green (993)

◣ Dark green (991)

Ⅱ Red brown (918)

◼ Black (310)

◿ Brown (839)

· Flesh (951)

⊞ Peach (758)

◺ Pink (962)

▲ Earth brown (300)

⊠ Rust brown (434)

⬤ Golden yellow (742)

1 Square = 1 Stitch

**Donkey**

**COLOR KEY**

⊘ Tan (841)

◼ Light rust (3064)

· Light gray (3072)

⊞ Black (310)

⊠ Brown (839)

1 Square = 1 Stitch

# CHRISTMAS CAROLS

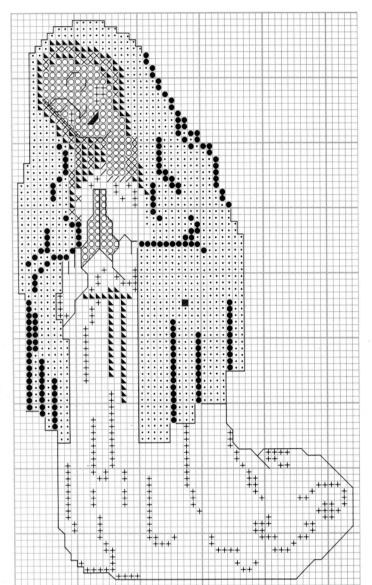

**Mary**

**COLOR KEY**

- ◉ Dark blue (797)
- · Light blue (809)
- ⊠ Rust brown (434)
- ◨ Brown (839)
- ○ Flesh (951)
- ◪ Golden yellow (742)
- ⊞ Peach (758)

**1 Square = 1 Stitch**

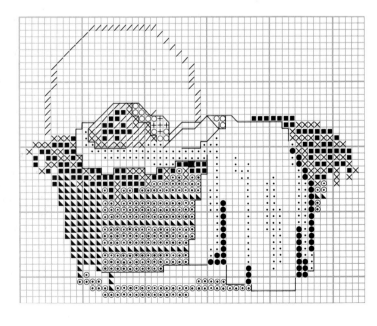

**Infant**

**COLOR KEY**

- ◪ Golden yellow (442)
- ◼ Yellow (726)
- ◉ Dark blue (797)
- · Light Blue (809)
- ⊠ Rust brown (434)
- ◨ Dark gray (414)
- ◉ Light gray (3072)
- ○ Flesh (951)
- ⊞ Peach (758)

**1 Square = 1 Stitch**

# Holly and Ivy Stocking

Shown on page 39.

Stocking is 17¾ inches tall.

## MATERIALS
DMC embroidery floss: 1 skein each of light teal (992), dark teal (991), lime green (906), light olive green (470), dark olive green (937), pink (893), dark coral (891), peach (352), brown (898), kelly green (911), gray green (503), off-white (3033)
14x22-inch piece of 14-count cream Aida cloth
¾ yard of moiré satin for backing, lining, and piping
2 yards of narrow cotton cording
Polyester fleece
Water-erasable pen
Tracing paper

## INSTRUCTIONS
Before beginning, see the general information on pages 78 and 79 for special cross-stitch tips and techniques, and for materials necessary for working all counted cross-stitch projects.

CROSS–STITCHING: Refer to the chart on page 50 and begin stitching at the top of the design, at the arrow, 2½ inches from the top edge, and 6 inches from the left edge of the fabric. Use 2 strands of floss to work cross-stitches over 1 thread of the fabric. Add the small motif to the bottom of the design. The shaded symbols are for placement only; do not work the shaded area.

ASSEMBLY: Enlarge and trace the stocking pattern, *right,* onto tracing paper; cut out stocking shape. Referring to photo, page 39, carefully align the traced stocking atop the stitched piece; secure in place. With the water-erasable pen, draw the stocking shape onto the fabric.

Cut stocking shape from Aida cloth, leaving ⅜-inch seam allowance. Cut another stocking piece from the satin fabric for backing and two more pieces for lining. Cut two more shapes from fleece. From the remaining piece of satin cut and piece 1½-inch-wide bias strips for piping.

Baste fleece to wrong sides of stitched piece and backing fabric.

Cover cording to make piping. With right sides facing, sew the piping to the cross-stitched piece around all edges.

With right sides together, sew stocking backing to front, leaving top edge free. Clip curves, turn and press.

With right sides facing, sew two lining pieces together, leaving top edge free; trim seams. Press under ⅜-inch seam along top edge. Insert lining inside stocking and hand-sew lining to the seam edge along top of stocking.

**Holly Stocking**

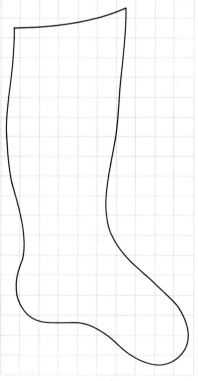

**1 Square = 1 Inch**

# Holly and Ivy Wreath

Shown on page 38.

Finished stitched wreath design is 20x20 inches.

## MATERIALS
31x31-inch piece of 11-count cream Aida cloth
DMC embroidery floss in the following amounts and colors: 2 skeins *each* of light teal (No. 992), dark teal (No. 991), light olive green (No. 470), and gray green (No. 503); 1 skein *each* of lime green (No. 906), dark olive green (No. 937), pink (No. 893), dark coral (No. 891), peach (No. 352), brown (No. 898), kelly green (No. 911), and off-white (No. 3033)
Graph paper
Colored felt tip pens

## INSTRUCTIONS
Before beginning, see the general information on pages 78 and 79 for special cross-stitch tips and techniques, and for materials necessary for working all counted cross-stitch projects.

The chart on page 51 represents one-fourth of the design. For best results, using colored pens, chart the complete design onto graph paper before you begin to stitch.

Begin charting at line A-B (9 o'clock) on the design and work to line C-D (12 o'clock). Working *clockwise,* chart design from A-B to C-D again (3 o'clock). Continue around in this manner two times more to complete the wreath. The shaded portions of the chart below the A-B line show how the shapes interlock as they scroll around the wreath. Do not chart the shaded portion.

Begin stitching the design 6¼ inches from the left edge of the fabric and 15½ inches from the top edge. Work in the same sequence as described for charting. Use two strands of floss to work cross-stitches over one thread of the cloth. When stitching is complete, frame as desired.

Begin stitching here

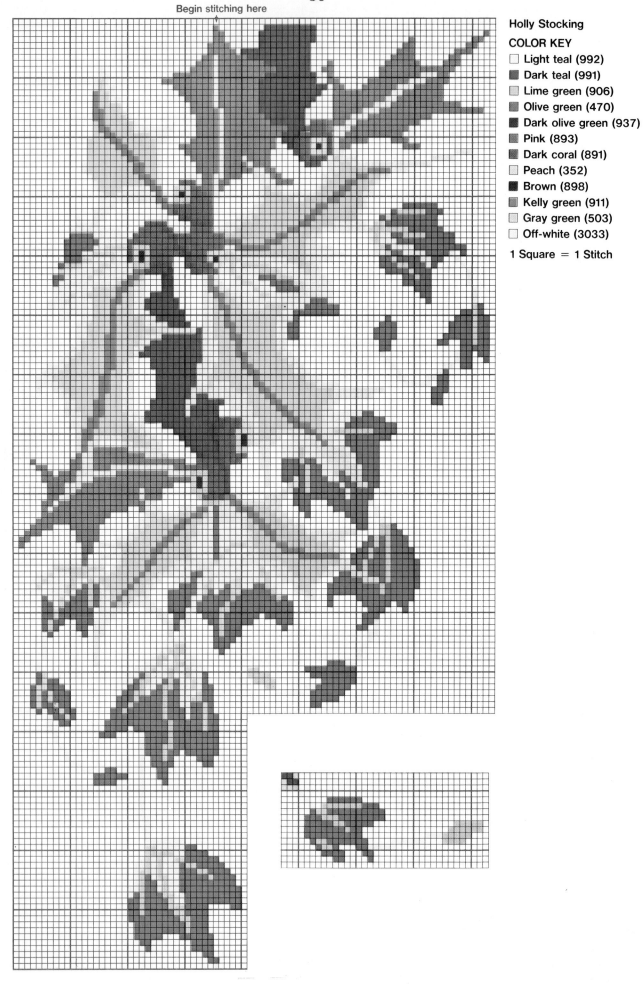

**Holly Stocking**

**COLOR KEY**

☐ Light teal (992)
■ Dark teal (991)
☐ Lime green (906)
■ Olive green (470)
■ Dark olive green (937)
■ Pink (893)
■ Dark coral (891)
☐ Peach (352)
■ Brown (898)
■ Kelly green (911)
☐ Gray green (503)
☐ Off-white (3033)

1 Square = 1 Stitch

# CHRISTMAS CAROLS

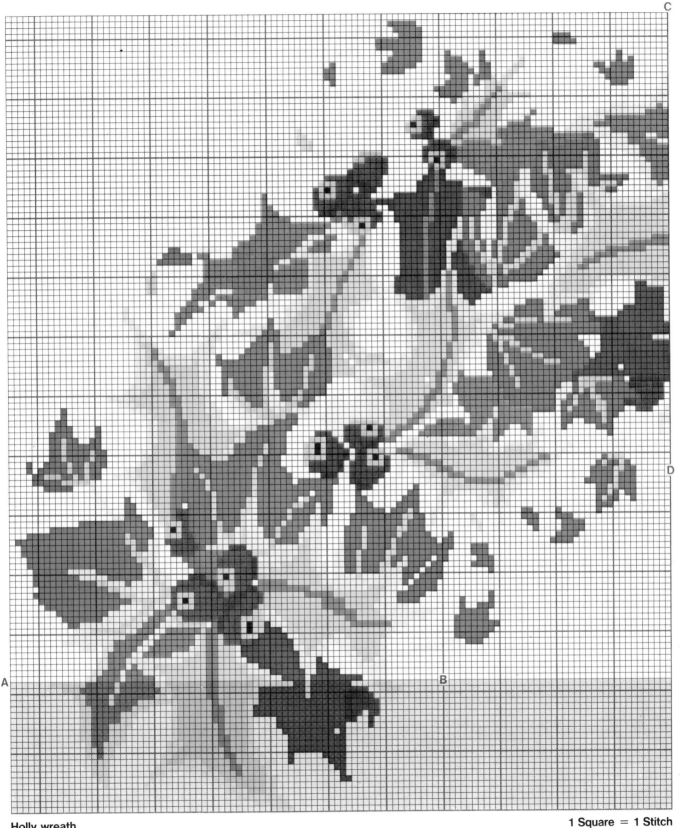

**Holly wreath**

1 Square = 1 Stitch

**COLOR KEY**

| | | |
|---|---|---|
| ☐ Light teal (992) | ☐ Lime green (906) | ☐ Peach (352) |
| ■ Dark teal (991) | ■ Dark olive green (937) | ■ Brown (898) |
| ■ Light olive green (470) | ■ Pink (893) | ■ Kelly green (911) |
| ☐ Gray green (503) | ■ Dark coral (891) | ☐ Off-white (3033) |

# Country Angel

Shown on page 41.

Angel stands approximately 14½ inches tall.

## MATERIALS

⅜ yard of 44-inch-wide muslin for head, skirt base, hands, and apron lining
⅓ yard of 44-inch-wide burgundy calico fabric for dress
⅜ yard of 44-inch-wide pink calico fabric for dress ruffle and bonnet
4x12-inch strip of pink pindot fabric for cap brim
10x12-inch rectangle of textured ecru fabric for wings
13x13-inch and 8x8-inch squares of ecru Davosa fabric for apron skirt and bib
Crystal Palace Country Silk (50-gram skein): 1 skein of beige tweed (No. 2101) for hair
Polyester fiberfill
Matching threads
1½ yards of ¼-inch-wide ecru lace for apron and wings trim
1 yard of ⅜-inch-wide ecru grosgrain ribbon for apron
¾ yard of ¼-inch-wide rose grosgrain ribbon for bonnet
1 yard of ¹⁄₁₆-inch-wide blue satin ribbon for skirt ruffle
Graph paper and felt-tip marking pens (optional)
DMC embroidery floss: 1 skein *each* of pink (No. 758), red (No. 347), burgundy (No. 814), light green (No. 503), dark green (No. 501), light brown (No. 420), dark brown (No. 3031), yellow (No. 726), blue (No. 932), and white
1 spool *each* of DMC silver and gold metallic embroidery threads for wings
Two 6-inch strands of florist wire for armature
Tissue paper
Dressmaker's carbon paper
Water-erasable pen
6-inch diameter cardboard circle
Small purchased basket

## INSTRUCTIONS

PREPARING THE PATTERNS: Trace patterns on pages 54–55 onto tissue paper.

*Note:* Seam allowances are *not* included on the head, apron bib, and apron skirt patterns. All other patterns and measurements include ¼ inch for seam allowances. Stitch all pattern pieces together with right sides facing unless otherwise noted.

CUTTING PATTERN PIECES: From the burgundy calico, cut out the dress bodice, sleeves, one 1½x8½-inch rectangle for skirt waistband, and one 8¼x30-inch rectangle for the skirt.

From the pink calico, cut out bonnet cap and one 5½x44-inch strip for the skirt ruffle.

From the pink pindot, cut out the bonnet brim.

Cut two 8½x14½-inch rectangles from the muslin for the doll body form. Cut one 10x10-inch square for the head front, and two 3½-inch-diameter circles for the hands.

### For the doll body

HEAD: Center the head pattern on page 57 atop the 10x10-inch square of muslin and trace her features in place using the water-erasable pen. Then, mount the fabric in the hoop.

Using 2 strands of floss, satin-stitch a red mouth, pink cheeks (hearts) and light brown eyes; use outline stitches for light brown eyelids. Press on the wrong side with a warm iron. Machine baste around the outline of the head.

Lay the embroidered head atop another muslin piece, right sides together; sew around head, leaving neck edge open. Trim away excess fabric and clip curves. Turn to right side and press. Stuff with fiberfill; set aside.

HAIR: Cut hank into 16-inch lengths. (We used approximately 250 strands for our doll's wig, but you may use more or less.) Cut a 1x3½-inch wig strip from muslin. Then center hair across strip; stitch in place down the center of the strip. Slip-stitch wig to head; trim yarn and clip bangs.

SLEEVES: Press under ¼-inch cuff seam twice; hem. Run gathering threads at cap of sleeve. Sew underarm seam. Turn sleeve to right side. Repeat for other sleeve.

BODICE: Sew front and back pieces together at shoulders, leaving neck edge open. Gather the sleeves to fit the armhole openings and sew in place. Sew the side seams from the waist to the shoulder edge, sewing closed the sleeve opening. Stuff the sleeves lightly with fiberfill or tissue paper for added crispness.

HANDS: Fold one muslin circle around a small amount of fiberfill. Wrap the circle with florist wire, leaving 4 inches of wire to slip into the sleeve for added shaping. Turn under ¼-inch cuff seam, insert wire into sleeve, and hand-sew sleeve to hand. Repeat for other hand.

SKIRT BASE: Sew the long sides of the muslin rectangles together. Gather one open edge to fit the calico bodice. With right sides together, sew the skirt base to the bodice.

Press under ½-inch seam allowance on skirt base; run gathering threads ⅛ and ¼ inch from edge. Firmly stuff skirt base and bodice with fiberfill. Insert cardboard base and pull gathering threads taut to form base for angel; secure threads.

### For the clothing

SKIRT RUFFLE: Press under the edges of the short sides of ruffle strip. Fold strip in half *lengthwise* with right sides facing; sew seam along raw edges. Turn to right side, press and hand-sew opening edges together to form a tube; press. Run a gathering thread ¼ inch from top edge of ruffle. Set ruffle aside.

SKIRT: Sew center back seam, leaving a 2½-inch opening at the top. Press back seam allowance of opening.

Gather ruffle to fit bottom edge of skirt; sew in place along skirt seam line. Slip-stitch narrow blue ribbon atop seam line of ruffle.

Gather top edge of skirt to fit waistband; gather *between* seam lines. Fold waistband in half *lengthwise*, right sides together; sew short edges; clip edges and turn. With sides facing, sew both raw edges of waistband to skirt. Turn waistband up.

Slip skirt over angel and secure at back waistband.

*continued*

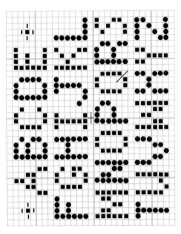

**Country Angel**

**COLOR KEY**
- ⊟ Pink (758)
- ⊠ Red (347)
- ■ Burgundy (814)
- ⊟ Light green (503)
- ● Dark green (501)
- ⊞ Light brown (420)
- ◀ Dark brown (3031)
- ◿ Yellow (726)
- ◯ Blue (932)
- · White
- ◣ Gold Metalic

**1 Square = 1 Stitch**

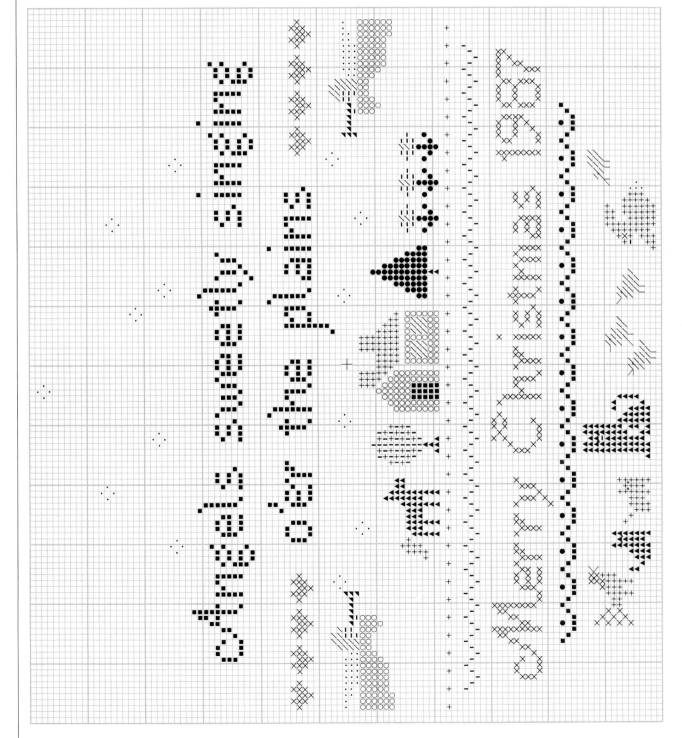

**APRON:** Referring to the chart on page 53, locate the center of the apron skirt cross-stitch pattern and the center of the large Davosa square; begin stitching there. Likewise, locate the center of the apron bib cross-stitch pattern and the center of the small Davosa square and begin stitching there.

Use two strands of floss or one strand of metallic thread to work each cross-stitch over one thread of the fabric. Work backstitches with light brown for the turkey's and chicks' beaks and the chicks' feet. Stitch French knots with light brown to work the turkey's and chicks' eyes; use red to work the bunny's eye; use blue to work the kitten's eyes.

When stitching is complete, lay tissue paper pattern atop each of the stitcheries. Trace pattern outlines onto Davosa using a water-erasable pen. Add ½-inch seams. Cut matching linings from the muslin.

Sew lace to curved edge of embroidered apron skirt and bib (do not add lace to bottom edge of bib). With right sides facing, sew linings to stitched skirt and bib, leaving openings at waist for turning. *Note:* Do not sew into seam allowance when sewing lining to bib at waist. Clip curves, turn to right side, and press.

Gather apron skirt to fit bib. With right sides facing, sew waist seams together, keeping lining of bib free. Slip-stitch bib lining over seam allowances at waist.

Cut a 5-inch length from the ⅜-inch ecru ribbon and tack in place at one corner of bib. Center and whipstitch remaining strip of ribbon to the lining along the waistline. Tie apron to angel. Loop ribbon around neck and secure other end to bib.

**BONNET:** Cut bonnet cap from pink calico. Fold bonnet in half *widthwise* with wrong sides together. Run a gathering thread ¼ inch from curved edge.

Gather bonnet cap to fit between seam lines of bonnet brim; sew in place. Press the raw edge

under ¼ inch. Fold brim in half, right sides facing, and stitch short ends. Turn to right side, press, and hand-sew the folded edge over the seam allowance.

To shape bonnet, stitch several tucks at the center back. Center and hand-sew pink grosgrain ribbon along the neck edge of the bonnet. Tie bonnet to head.

**WINGS:** Transfer one wing pattern for wing front to textured ecru fabric using dressmaker's carbon paper. Then, back with a layer of batting. Do not cut out.

Mount fabric in an embroidery hoop and quilt the marked lines using four strands of pink floss. Using a single strand of silver thread, fill in areas with an overall quilt pattern of diagonal squares or another quilt pattern of your choice. Border wings with lace, leaving top edge untrimmed.

Cut a second wing pattern from ecru fabric for backing. Sew front wings to backing, leaving an opening for turning. Clip curves, turn to right side, and press. Stuff wings lightly with fiberfill. Slip-stitch the opening closed. Stitch wings to back of angel.

Place basket over angel's arm.

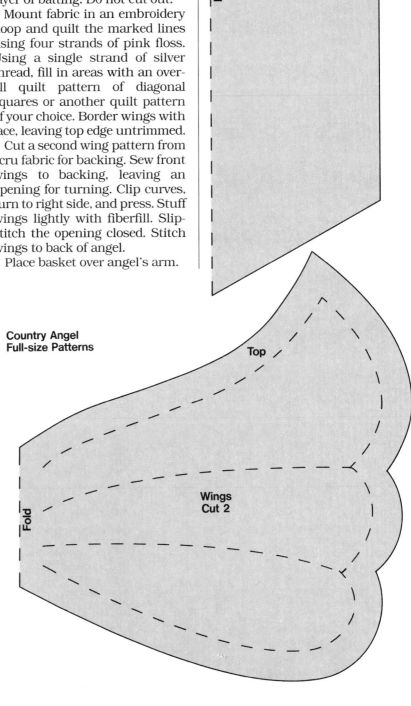

Fold

**Bonnet Brim**
**Cut 1**

Fold

**Country Angel**
**Full-size Patterns**

Top

Fold

**Wings**
**Cut 2**

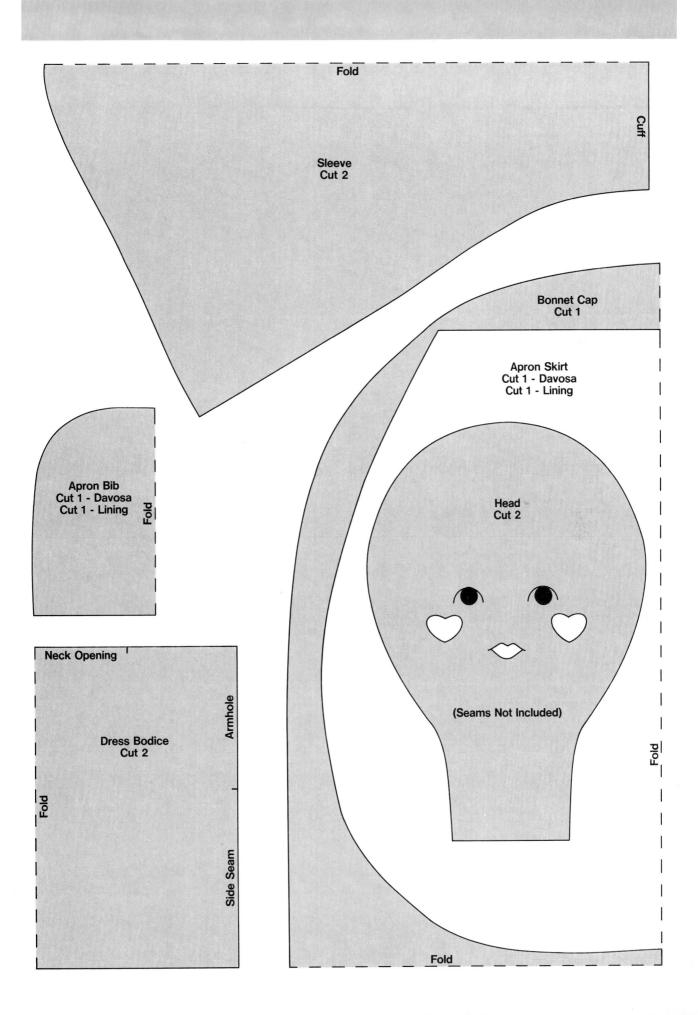

Fold

Sleeve
Cut 2

Cuff

Bonnet Cap
Cut 1

Apron Skirt
Cut 1 - Davosa
Cut 1 - Lining

Apron Bib
Cut 1 - Davosa
Cut 1 - Lining

Fold

Head
Cut 2

(Seams Not Included)

Neck Opening

Armhole

Dress Bodice
Cut 2

Fold

Side Seam

Fold

Fold

Begin stitching here →

**Santa Stocking**

1 Square = 1 Stitch

**COLOR KEY**

| | | | | |
|---|---|---|---|---|
| ⊡ Beige (738) | ◪ Charcoal (317) | ◣ Peach (754) | ◍ Blue (798) | ⊠ Yellow (973) |
| ◎ Burgundy (816) | ⊟ Cream (739) | ⊠ Gray (415) | ◉ Rose (603) | ⊞ Dark blue (797) | ◩ Light brown (437) |
| ◼ Red (666) | ◥ Brown (433) | ◿ Pink (605) | ⊡ Green (699) | ● Purple (552) | ◪ Black (310) |

# Santa Stocking

Shown on page 42.

Stocking is 17½ inches tall.

## MATERIALS
16x18 piece of white hardanger
DMC embroidery floss, 1 skein *each* of the following colors: burgundy (No. 816), red (No. 666), beige (No. 738), cream (No. 739), brown (No. 433)
Scraps of charcoal (No. 317), gray (No. 415), pink (No. 605), peach (No. 754), rose (No. 603), green (No. 699), blue (No. 798), dark blue (No. 797), purple (No. 552), yellow (No. 973), light brown (No. 437), and black (No. 310)
Angora yarn, 1 ounce ball
DMC pearl cotton, Size 5, 1 skein of red
Small bell, small wooden red bead, narrow red and green ribbons, and purchased appliqués and toy buttons for Santa's bag
½ yard red cotton fabric for backing and cuff
¾ yard green pindot cotton fabric for piping and lining
2 yards cotton cording
½ yard polyester fleece

## INSTRUCTIONS
Before beginning, see the general information on pages 78 and 79 for special cross-stitch tips and techniques, and for materials necessary for working all counted cross-stitch projects.

STITCHING THE STOCKING: Referring to chart, *at left,* begin stitching at the top of Santa's hat 2½ inches from the top edge and 5 inches from the right edge of the fabric. Work the stitches over two threads of the hardanger, using two strands of floss.

Work the backstitches on Santa's beard and fur trim on his suit with one strand of charcoal. Use red backstitches to outline large package and green to outline small package. Work fur on Santa's suit and hat with *half-crosses,* using one strand of angora

yarn. Brush angora with small brush to work up nap of yarn.

When all stitching is complete, press on wrong side.

Make 2 braided cords from pearl cotton (see how-to for Plaid Ornaments, page 15, for making braid), using 48 inches of thread for each tie. Weave ties along edge of Santa's pack and tie at center.

Referring to photo on page 42, embellish stocking as follows: Sew bell to Santa's hat, sew bead to end of train string for pull, tie small bows and tack atop packages and at neck of bear. Trim appliqués to fit edge of Santa's bag and sew in place. Sew toy buttons to fill in spaces as desired.

ASSEMBLY: Enlarge stocking pattern, *right,* onto tracing paper and center atop stitching; pin in place. Adding ⅜-inch seam allowances, cut out stocking shape. Cut one stocking shape from red fabric and two from pindot fabric for lining. Cut two stocking shapes from fleece.

For the cuff, cut two 6x18-inch strips from the red fabric and one strip to match from the fleece.

Baste fleece to wrong sides of the stitched piece, the red backing, and one cuff piece.

Cover the cording with green pindot for piping. Sew piping to right side of stitched stocking along seam line and along one long edge of the fleece-backed cuff.

With right sides together, sew stocking front to back, leaving top edge free; clip corners.

Sew two cuff pieces together, right sides facing, along edge with piping. Then open and fold in half *lengthwise* and sew two sides together to make a tube; clip seams, turn, and press. Pin and sew cuff to wrong side of stocking top edge. Turn stocking right side out; fold cuff over to right side of stocking.

With right sides together, sew lining pieces together; trim seams and clip curves. Insert lining into stocking; fold back seam allowance and hand-sew in place along top seam allowance.

**Santa Stocking**

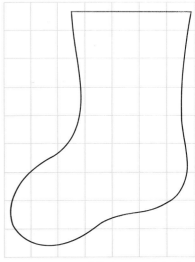

1 Square = 2 Inches

# Santa's Treat Sack

Shown on page 43.

Finished sack is 12 inches high.

## MATERIALS
9x9½-inch piece of 11-count Aida Cloth
DMC embroidery floss in the following amounts and colors: 1 skein of red (No. 666); scraps of peach (No. 754), burgundy (No. 816), charcoal (No. 317), gray (No. 415), pink (No. 605), rose (No. 603), green (No. 699), and blue (No. 798)
⅜ yard green cotton fabric
⅜ yard red print cotton fabric
Fusible webbing
Small jingle bell
⅔ yard red soutache

## INSTRUCTIONS
Before beginning, see the general information on pages 78 and 79 for special cross-stitch tips and techniques.

CROSS–STITCHING SANTA'S FACE: Referring to chart on page 58, locate the center of the design and the center of the Aida cloth; begin stitching there. Use two strands of floss to work the cross-stitches over one thread of the Aida cloth. Work the backstitches
*continued*

around Santa's beard and the fur trim on his hat with charcoal-colored floss.

ASSEMBLING THE BAG: From the two contrasting fabrics, cut rectangles 12¾x22 inches. At the center front of the green fabric and 1¼ inches up from the bottom edge, draw a 5x5¾-inch rectangle. Machine-stitch atop the drawn line. Cut out the rectangle, leaving ¼ inch of fabric inside the rectangle; clip into corners. Press ¼-inch seams to wrong side.

Center the stitched piece on the wrong side of the opening and baste in place. Trim seam allowance of stitchery to ¼ inch. To frame the stitchery, sew soutache atop the folded edge through all thicknesses.

With wrong sides facing, fuse the green fabric to the red print fabric using the fusible webbing. Overlap the two short sides 1 inch (center back) and fuse the two edges together. Fold the bag in half, with lining side facing itself, and press the two sides to make sharp folds. Stitch along both of the side edges ⅛ inch from the folds to within 2 inches from the bottom edges.

From the two fabrics, cut 4x6-inch rectangles for bottom of sack; fuse together. With right sides facing, sew bottom piece to bag top, using ¼-inch seam allowance; turn.

Fold the bag to establish its shape; press firmly to form the triangular lines (on sides) inward.

Trim top of bag with pinking shears. Cut out the half-circle with plain shears.

Sew bell to Santa's hat.

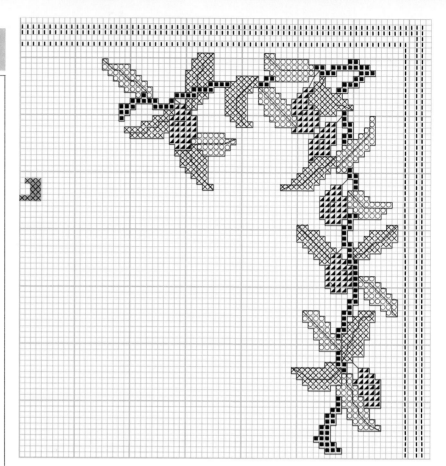

Twelve Days of Christmas Sampler - Upper Right          1 Square = 1 Stitch

**Santa Treat Sack**

**COLOR KEY**
- ■ Red (666)
- ◣ Peach (754)
- ◯ Burgundy (816)
- ◿ Charcoal (317)
- ⊠ Gray (415)
- ⬚ Pink (605)
- ● Rose (603)
- ⋅ Green (699)
- ⊞ Blue (798)

1 Square = 1 Stitch

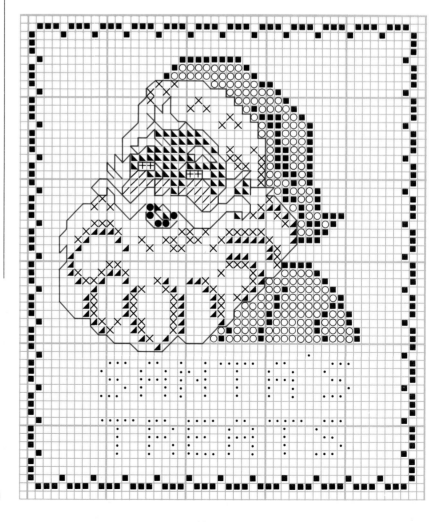

ON THE
FIRST DAY
OF CHRISTMAS
MY TRUE LOVE GAVE
TO ME-A PARTRIDGE IN A
PEAR TREE, ON THE SECOND DAY
OF CHRISTMAS MY TRUE
LOVE GAVE TO ME-2 TURTLE
DOVES,ON THE THIRD DAY OF CHRIST-
MAS MY TRUE LOVE GAVE TO ME-3 FRENCH
HENS, ON THE FOURTH DAY OF CHRISTMAS MY
TRUE LOVE GAVE TO ME-4 CALLING BIRDS, ON THE
FIFTH DAY OF CHRISTMAS MY TRUE LOVE

**Twelve Days of Christmas Sampler**                    **1 Square = 1 Stitch**

## COLOR KEY
- ⊞ Loden green (934)
- ⊙ Dark green (904)
- ⊠ Light green (905)
- ▣ Dark brown (801)
- ◣ Light brown (434)
- ● Coral (758)
- ⊞ Olive brown (370)
- ⊡ Yellow (725)
- ⊟ Cream (677)
- ◪ Gold Metalic

# Twelve Days of Christmas Sampler

Shown on page 45.

Finished size of stitched piece is 16¾x22 inches.

### MATERIALS
24x30-inch piece of white hardanger

DMC embroidery floss in the following colors: 3 skeins of loden green (No. 934); 2 skeins of olive green (No. 730); 1 skein *each* of dark green (No. 904), light green (No. 905), and brown (No. 801)

Scraps of light brown (No. 434), coral (No. 758), olive brown (No. 370), yellow (No. 725), and cream (No. 677)

10 yards of gold metallic thread
Small red, yellow, blue, and green glass beads

*continued*

GAVE TO ME-5 GOLDEN

DAY OF CHRISTMAS MY T

GEESE A LAYING, ON THE SE

MY TRUE LOVE GAVE TO ME- 7

EIGHTH DAY OF CHRISTMAS MY

A MILKING, ON THE NINTH D

LOVE GAVE TO ME-9 LADIES O

CHRISTMAS MY TRUE LOVE GAVE

THE ELEVENTH DAY OF CHRISTMA

PIPERS PIPING,ON THE TWELFTH DA

TO ME

DRUM

DRUM

STITCHED BY

**Twelve Days of Christmas Sampler**                                    **Lower Left**

## INSTRUCTIONS

Before beginning, see the general information on pages 78 and 79 for special cross-stitch tips and techniques.

Begin stitching the border in the upper left-hand corner 3½ inches from the top edge and 4 inches from the side edge of the cloth. Use two strands of floss to work the cross-stitches over two threads of the hardanger. Work 188 stitches across the *top*, then work 242 stitches *down* the right side edge (a total of 243 stitches from top to bottom); complete the remaining two sides to match. The charts, *above*, show how the remaining border stitches are worked.

Referring to chart on page 58, work the branch motif in the upper right-hand corner; then work the mirror image in the left-hand corner. Use one ply of metallic thread over two threads of fabric to work the cross-stitches of pears. *Note:* Shaded portion on this chart is for placement of the partridge motif on chart, page 59.

When the corner motifs are completed, work the shaded area (top leaf) on the chart to establish a starting point for the partridge motif. Then refer to chart on page 59 to complete the whole motif and the top portion of the tree.

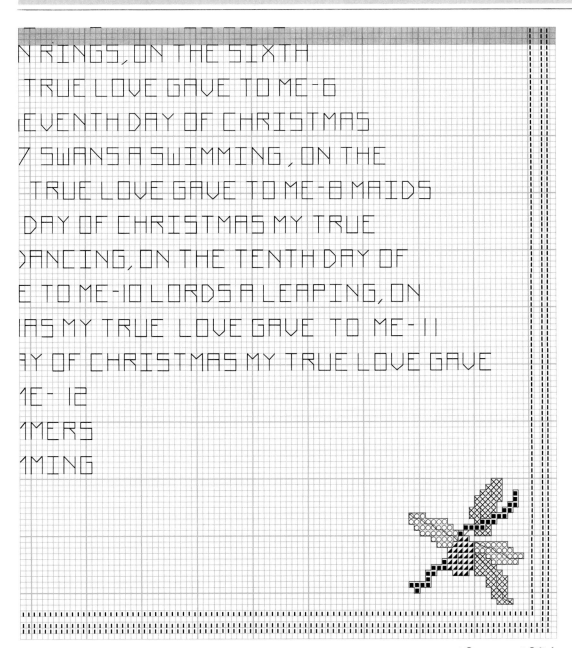

N RINGS, ON THE SIXTH

TRUE LOVE GAVE TO ME-6

EVENTH DAY OF CHRISTMAS

7 SWANS A SWIMMING, ON THE

TRUE LOVE GAVE TO ME-8 MAIDS

DAY OF CHRISTMAS MY TRUE

DANCING, ON THE TENTH DAY OF

E TO ME-10 LORDS A LEAPING, ON

AS MY TRUE LOVE GAVE TO ME-11

AY OF CHRISTMAS MY TRUE LOVE GAVE

1E-12

1MERS

1MING

**Lower Right**                    **1 Square = 1 Stitch**

Work the backstitching of the tree verse with two strands of olive green. Complete the tree following chart, *opposite*, for the lower left side, and chart, *above*, for the lower right side. Use dark brown to backstitch the verse for the trunk. *Note:* The shaded areas on these charts are for placement only and show stitches already worked. Do not work these areas.

Use loden green for backstitching around the pears, leaves, branches, and bird. With loden green work half-crosses for pear stems and a French knot at tip of partridge's plummage.

Stitch your name and date in space below trunk. (Chart your name onto graph paper and center the "stitched by" line onto the chart before stitching).

Work the balls of the tree by stitching 6 glass beads to *each* of the O's on the tree.

Frame as desired.

# A NEW ENGLAND
# CHRISTMAS SAMPLER

❖❖❖

**Welcome to New England, the birthplace of American history, lasting traditions, and sumptuous country charm. To help you recall earlier times, here is a chapter filled with sampler projects—delightful heritage Christmas gifts and trims—that will add to your family's Christmas this year and for years to come.**

◆

The unique cross-stitch tree sampler, *opposite,* greets the season and sets the stage for a yule-time celebration. Stitched with embroidery floss on hardanger, this 23x25 inch sampler is full of rows of traditional cross-stitch sampler motifs and holiday sayings.

To complete this masterful sampler,

surround it with the tree-shaped mat board by following the instructions provided, or take it to a professional framer.

More gift and trim ideas using these sampler motifs are on the next four pages. Instructions for all the projects in this chapter begin on page 68.

Re-create the sayings and motifs of the cross-stitch sampler on the previous page to deck your fresh evergreen.

The giant cross-stitch banners festooned with ribbons and the simple motif ornaments, *opposite*, will captivate your friends and heartily welcome them to a holiday celebration. You might even drape the banners across doorways or your fireplace mantel.

Cross-stitched on burlap with woolen yarns, these tree trims are quick and easy enough for even a child to stitch. Outline the designs with colorful pipings and back with burlap or muslin when the stitching is complete.

If your tree doesn't rise to the ceiling, you can stitch these decorations with pearl cotton thread over one or two squares of 14-count Aida cloth. Your projects then will be reduced in size and can better match the scale of your tree.

And why not treat a special little miss with this huggable 18-inch-tall doll, *above*. Golden braids, wispy bangs, and a charming face add lots of personality that small tots will find irresistible come Christmas morning.

Stitched with woolen yarns on hardanger, this child-pleasing doll uses a rearrangement of the sampler motifs. A calico print backing and piping set off her homespun look and outline her attire and sweet girlish figure.

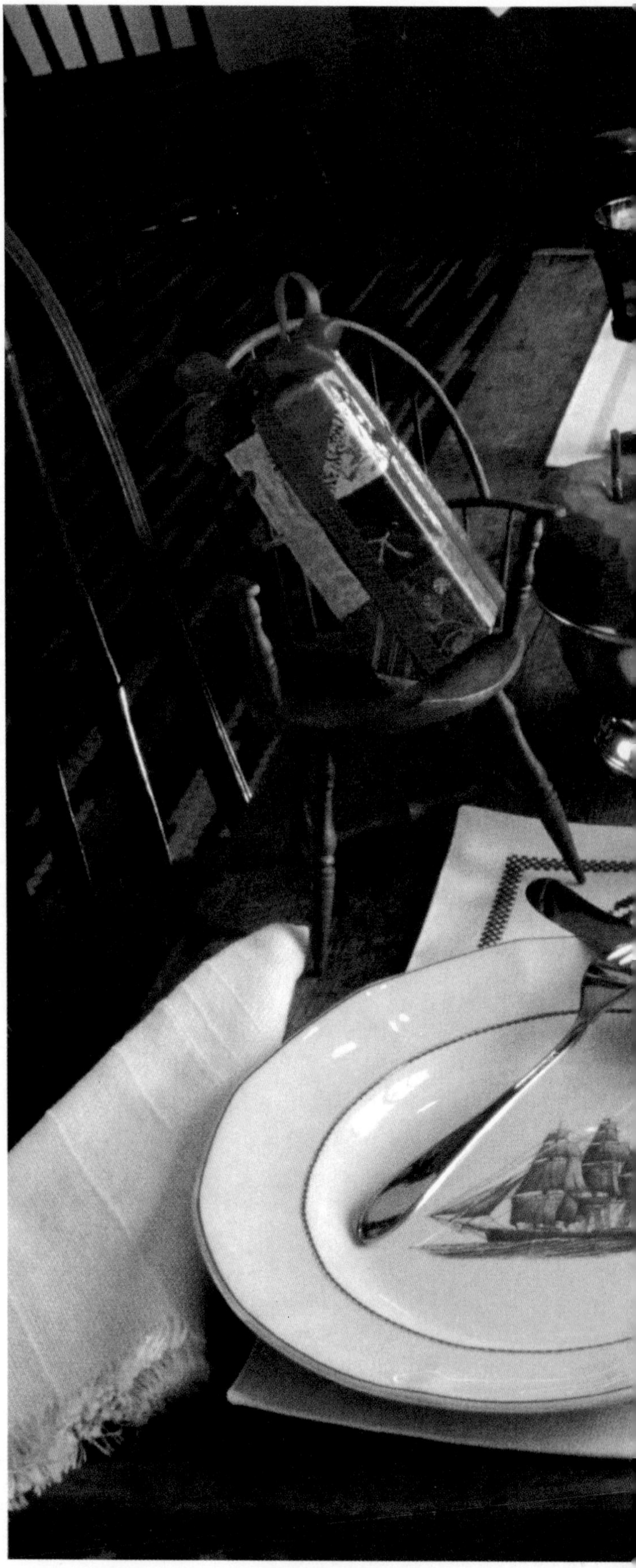

Ｎew Englanders, like other Americans, prize their heritage and time-honored traditions. And hanging Christmas stockings is among the best-loved of these holiday traditions.

Adapted from the motifs of the tree sampler, the 22½-inch-tall sampler stockings, *above,* are quick to stitch with wool yarns onto a 14-count even-weave fabric. We used Fiddler's cloth for a homespun look. Festive piping and muslin backing complete these one-of a kind stockings.

Ｇreet your dinner guests with this striking place mat set designed especially for joyful entertaining.

Stitched with embroidery floss onto hardanger, these 15x22 inch mats are a splendid rearrangement of the tree sampler motifs. For added crispness, line them with muslin or a fabric of your choice. To coordinate these tabletop accessories, you can use waste canvas to stitch sampler motifs onto purchased napkins as we did for the plaid place mats on pages 6 and 7.

## New England Tree Sampler

Shown on page 62.

Finished size of framed stitchery is 24x25 inches.

**MATERIALS**
28x29-inch piece of ecru hardanger
DMC embroidery floss, 1 skein *each* of the following colors: evergreen (No. 3345), jade green (No. 320), apple green (No. 3348), red (No. 349), dark brown (No. 300), light brown (No. 841), burgundy (No. 815), yellow (No. 726), light blue (No. 334), dark blue (No. 312), light gray (No. 415), dark gray (No. 413); scraps of pink (No. 963) and orange (No. 900)
Crafts knife; crafts glue
Two 22x23-inch mat boards in colors of your choice (1 light and 1 dark colored)

**INSTRUCTIONS**
Before beginning, see the general information on pages 78 and 79 for special cross-stitch tips and techniques, and for materials necessary for working all counted cross-stitch projects.

STITCHING THE TREE: Referring to the chart on page 69, begin stitching in the center of the star motif on the top of the tree 5 inches from the *center top edge* of the fabric. Use two strands of floss to work over two threads of the hardanger. Refer to charts on pages 70 and 71 for working the left and right sides of the lower portions of the tree. The shaded portions on these two charts are shown for placement only and represent stitches already completed. Do not stitch the shaded portions.

Work backstitches with two strands of orange to work beaks of birds; use dark brown to work legs of birds atop trees; use pink to work the backstitches on the rabbits.

Stitch masts of the ships with backstitches using two strands of dark brown; work long stitches using single strand of dark brown to add ropes for sails.

MATTING THE SAMPLER: You can take your stitchery to a framer to have the mats cut as shown on the photo, page 62, or follow the instructions below for cutting your own mat boards.

Enlarge the tree pattern, *below,* onto paper; cut out. Center and draw the tree outline onto the dark colored mat board. Use the crafts knife to cut out the tree. Cut the light mat board ⅜ inch beyond the original pattern; save the cutout.

ASSEMBLY: Center and glue the mat boards together. With the mat facedown on a table, center the stitchery over the tree-shaped hole; top with the batting. Fit the tree cutout into the hole to fasten the stitchery and batting in place. Run a line of glue along the cutout edges. Trim away excess fabric. Frame as desired.

**Tree Sampler Mat**

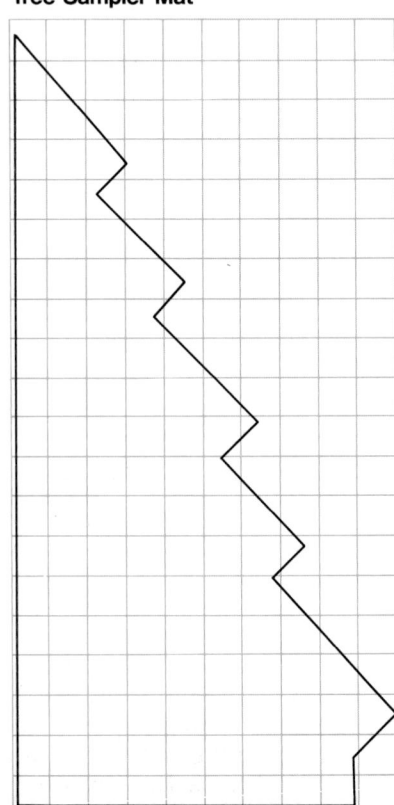

**1 Square = 1 Inch**

## Christmas Tree Banners

Shown on page 64.

**MATERIALS**
1¼ yards of 54-inch ecru burlap
Paternayan 3-ply Persian yarns in the following amounts and colors: 8 strands of lime green (No. 631), 12 strands of evergreen (No. 610), and 17 strands of red (No. 842) for the sayings on the banners; 14 strands of dark blue (No. 581), 3 strands of light blue (No. 552), 10 strands of yellow (No. 703), 3 strands of green (No. 612), and 2 strands of orange (No. 800) for the motifs on one banner
1¼ yards of 44-inch-wide muslin
1½ yards of stiff nonwoven interfacing
9 yards of purchased ecru or white piping
12 yards of ⅜-inch-wide red ribbon for bows on banners

**INSTRUCTIONS**
FOR THE MERRY CHRISTMAS BANNER: From the burlap, cut one 9x33-inch strip. Referring to the chart on page 69 for the Tree Sampler, begin stitching at the base of the "h" in the center of the burlap 3½ inches from the bottom edge of the strip. Use 3 plies of the lime green yarn to work the cross-stitches over 4 threads of the burlap. Work all letters from chart to complete the stitching. Trim the strip to measure 6x30 inches. Cut muslin and interfacing strips to match the stitched burlap strip.

FINISHING: Baste interfacing to wrong side of stitchery. Using ½-inch seam allowances, sew piping along outside edges. With right sides facing, sew muslin to stitched piece, leaving an opening for turning. Clip corners, turn and press. Tie ribbon bows to each end.

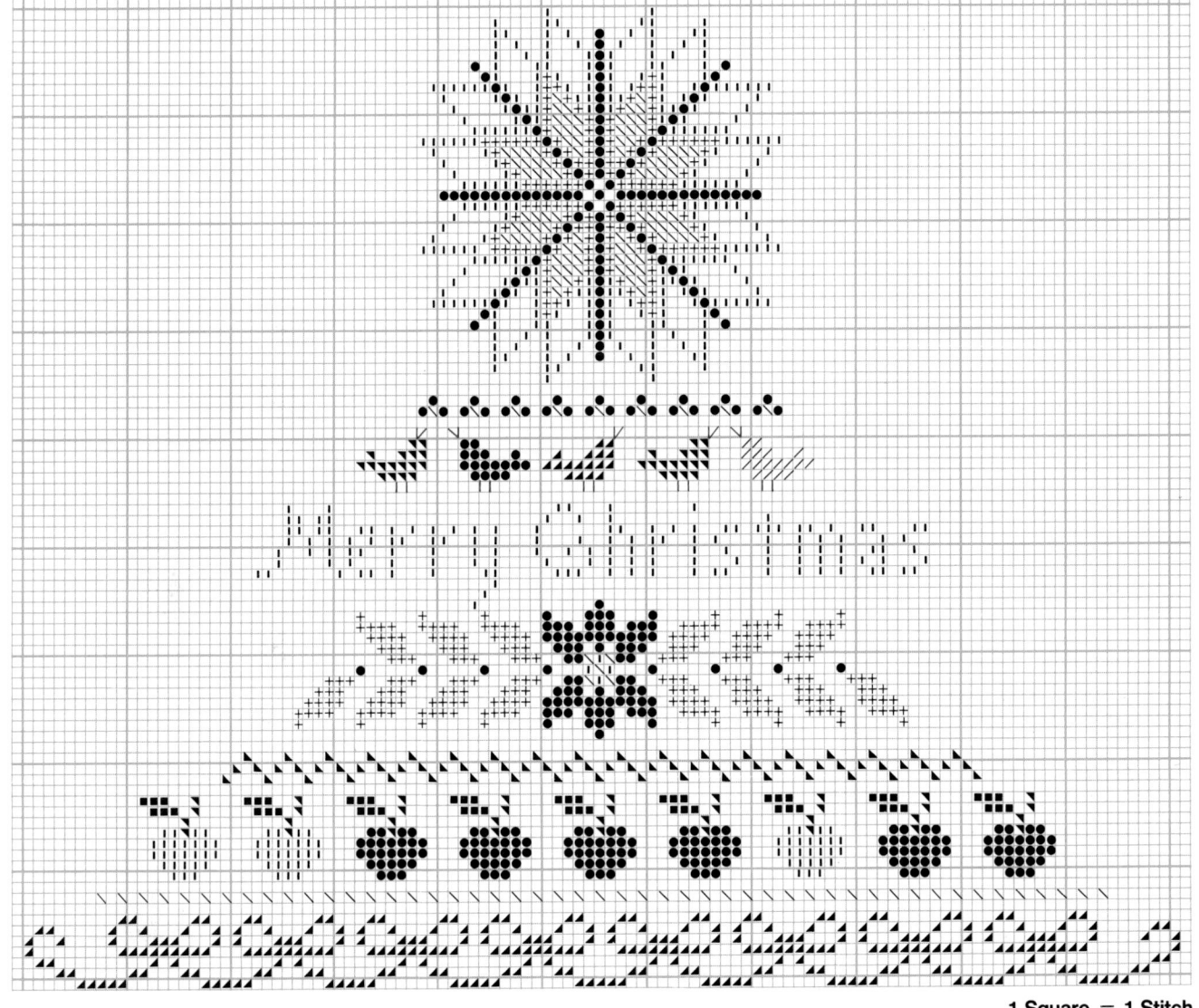

1 Square = 1 Stitch

**New England Tree Sampler-Top**

LOVE AND JOY BANNER: Cut one 9½x45-inch strip from the burlap. Begin stitching the tail of the "y" in "joy" 1½ inches to the left of the center of the burlap and 2½ inches from the bottom edge of the strip. Use 3 plies of the evergreen yarn to work the cross-stitches over 4 threads of the burlap. When all stitching is complete, trim the strip to measure 6½x42 inches. Cut muslin and interfacing strips to match the stitched strip. Follow Finishing instructions for Merry Christmas Banner, *opposite,* to complete.

PEACE ON EARTH BANNER: Cut and piece one 13x62-inch strip from burlap. Begin stitching the "o" in "on" 1½ inches to the left of the center of the burlap and 6 inches from the top edge of the strip. Use three plies of yarn to work the cross-stitches over four threads of the burlap. When the stitching is complete, trim the strip to measure 10x59-inches. Cut muslin and interfacing strips to match the stitched piece. Follow the Finishing instructions for Merry Christmas Banner, *opposite,* to complete.

**COLOR KEY**
■ Evergreen (3345)
⊞ Jade green (320)
⊡ Apple green (3348)
● Red (349)
◣ Dark brown (300)
◪ Light brown (841)
◣ Burgundy (815)
◻ Yellow (726)
◢ Light blue (334)
◎ Dark blue (312)
◤ Light gray (415)
⊡ Dark gray (413)
⊟ Pink (963)
▲ Orange (900)

**Lower Right**

1 Square = 1 Stitch

**COLOR KEY**

| | | | |
|---|---|---|---|
| ▣ | Evergreen (3345) | ◹ | Yellow (726) |
| ⊞ | Jade green (320) | ◿ | Light blue (334) |
| ⊡ | Apple green (3348) | ⊙ | Dark blue (312) |
| ⬤ | Red (349) | ◤ | Light gray (415) |
| ◥ | Dark brown (300) | ⊡ | Dark gray (413) |
| ⧄ | Light brown (841) | ⊟ | Pink (963) |
| ◣ | Burgundy (815) | ▲ | Orange (900) |

## Sampler Place Mat

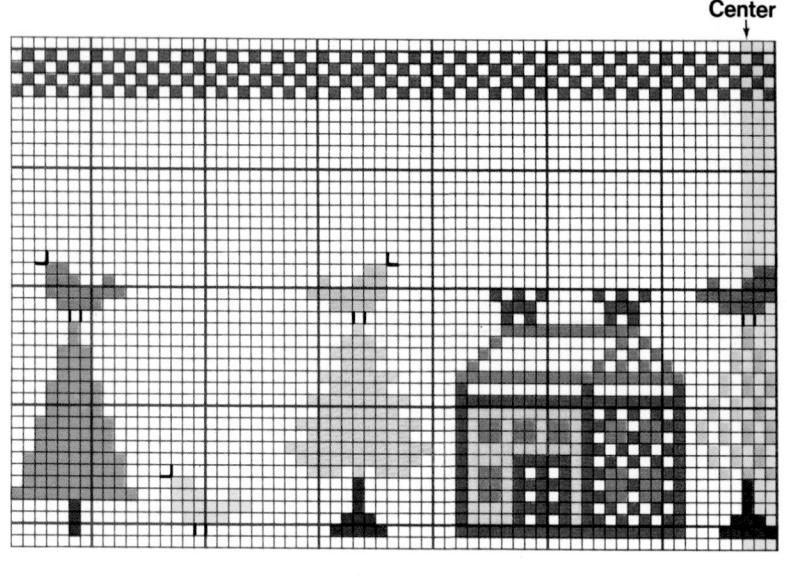

Center

Shown on page 66–67.

The finished size of one mat is 15x22 inches.

### MATERIALS
**For one place mat**
17x24-inch of ivory hardanger
DMC embroidery floss in the
following amounts and colors:
3 skeins *each* of evergreen
(No. 3345) and burgundy (No.
815); 2 skeins of red (No.
349); 1 skein *each* of jade
green (No. 320), apple green
(No. 3348), dark brown (No.
300), light brown (No. 841),
yellow (No. 726), light blue
(No. 334), dark blue (No. 312),
orange (No. 900), light gray
(No. 415), dark gray (No. 413)
16x23-inch piece of cotton
batiste for lining
Graph paper

### INSTRUCTIONS

Before beginning, see the general information on pages 78 and 79 for special cross-stitch tips and techniques, and for materials necessary for working all counted cross-stitch projects.

PREPARING THE STITCHING PATTERN: Chart the design, *opposite,* onto graph paper before beginning your stitching as follows. *Note:* The shaded areas on the chart on page 72 are for placement only; do not rechart them onto the graph paper.

Working from the center, chart the house and tree motifs across the top of the design to complete the top inside border strip. Chart the right side and its mirror image to the left of the basket to complete the left side of the middle strip. For the bottom strip, the design for the "love and joy come to you" message is given on the pattern; complete the ribbon border around this saying by charting the mirror image of the right side border. Then chart the mirror image of the apple motifs to

complete the left side of this strip. Make a mirror image of the vertical poinsettia design on the left side. Then complete the outside borders on the left side to match the right side.

STITCHING THE MAT: Begin stitching with the center stitch of the basket 8¼ inches from the *center top edge* of the hardanger. Use 3 strands of floss to work the cross-stitches over 2 threads of the fabric.

Work backstitches with two strands of orange to work beaks of birds; use dark brown to work legs of birds atop trees.

Stitch masts of the ships with backstitches, using two strands of dark brown; work long stitches using single strand of dark brown to add ropes for sails.

When all stitching is complete, press on wrong sides. Cut the mat to measure 16x23 inches leaving 1½-inch unstitched borders all around.

ASSEMBLY: With right sides facing and using ½-inch seam allowances, sew lining to stitched mat. Leave a 4-inch opening for turning. Trim seams, turn, and press. Edge-stitch around perimeter of entire mat.

**Sampler Place Mat**

### COLOR KEY
| | |
|---|---|
| ■ Evergreen (3345) | ▨ Yellow (726) |
| ■ Burgundy (815) | □ Light blue (334) |
| ■ Red (349) | ▨ Dark blue (312) |
| □ Jade green (320) | ■ Orange (900) |
| □ Apple green (3348) | □ Light gray (415) |
| ■ Dark brown (300) | ▨ Dark gray (413) |
| □ Light brown (841) | |

**1 Square = 1 Stitch**

Center

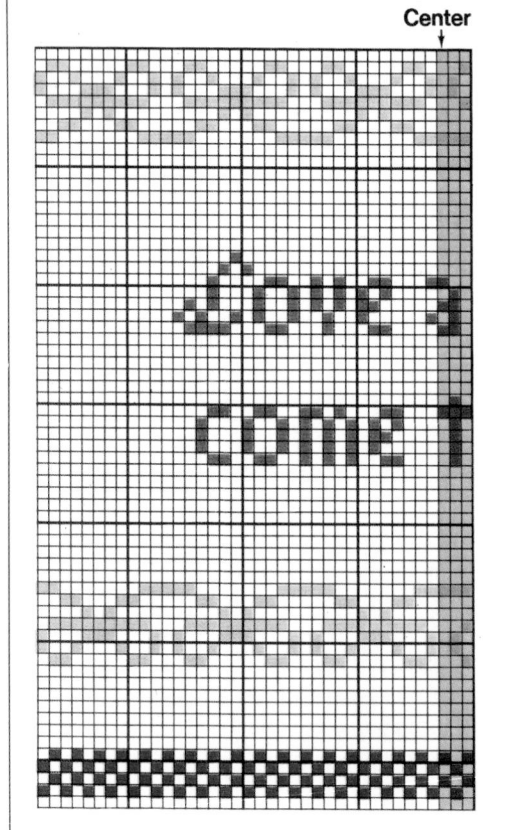

**Center**

**Sampler Placemat**

1 Square = 1 Stitch

## Sampler Ornaments

Shown on page 64.

**MATERIALS**
7- and 9- inch square scraps of
   ecru burlap
Scraps of Paternayan 3-ply
   Persian yarns in colors of
   your choice
Muslin and interfacing scraps
Purchased piping
Polyester fiberfill

**INSTRUCTIONS**
   Using motifs on Tree Sampler,
pages 69–71, cross-stitch the designs onto burlap using three
strands of yarn to work over four
threads of the fabric.
   When stitching is complete, cut
around shapes leaving ½-inch
seam allowances. Cut muslin and
interfacing to match cut shapes.
Baste interfacing to wrong side of

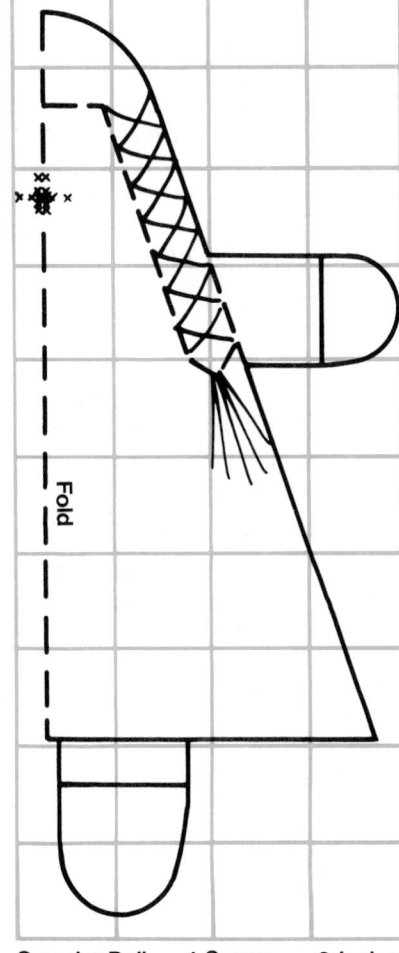

**Sampler Doll     1 Square = 2 Inches**

stitchery. Sew piping along seam
allowance. With right sides facing, sew stitchery to muslin, leaving an opening for turning. Turn,
stuff, and sew opening closed.

## Sampler Doll

Shown on page 65.

Finished doll is 18½ inches tall.

**MATERIALS**
18x22-inch piece of ivory
   hardanger
3-ply Paternayan Persian yarn
   in the following amounts and
   colors: 10 strands of red (No.
   842), 4 strands *each* of royal
   blue (No. 551) and gold (No.
   702); 3 strands of evergreen
   (No. 610); 2 strands *each* of
   lime green (No. 631) and light
   brown (No. 731); 1 strand
   *each* of dark brown (No. 410),
   cranberry (No. 940), and pink
   (No. 946)
¾ yard calico cotton fabric for
   backing and piping
2 yards narrow cotton cording
¾ yard ⅝-inch-wide blue ribbon
1 skein of yellow rug yarn for
   hair
4½-inch strip of yellow seam
   tape
Polyester fiberfill
Tracing paper
Water-erasable pen

**INSTRUCTIONS**
   Before beginning, see the general information on pages 78 and
79 for special cross-stitch tips
and techniques, and for materials
necessary for working all counted
cross-stitch projects.

   STITCHING THE DOLL: Referring to the chart on page 75, *top,
right,* begin stitching with the
face design at the nose 5½ inches
from the *center* top edge of the
fabric. *On the face only,* use one
ply of yarn to work the cross-
stitches over two threads of the
hardanger.
   Chart the diagram, *bottom,
right,* for the dress onto graph paper to make the mirror image of

the dress. *Note:* Begin the mirror
image one symbol to the left of the
centerline; do not repeat the center row of the chart. Refer to photo on page 65 for yarn colors for
the band of apple motifs.
   Mark off and leave unworked
20 threads below the bottom row
of the mouth; begin stitching the
neckline border at the center of
the design. Use two plies of yarn
to work cross-stitches over four
threads of the hardanger for the
remaining portions of the doll.
When all cross-stitching is complete, press on wrong side.

   ASSEMBLY: Enlarge and trace
pattern for doll, *left,* onto tracing
paper; cut out doll shape. Referring to photo, page 65, carefully
align the traced pattern atop the
stitched piece. With the water-
erasable pen, draw the doll shape
onto the fabric.
   Cut doll from hardanger, leaving ⅜-inch seam allowance. Cut
another piece to match from calico for backing.
   Cut 1-inch-wide bias strips of
calico; piece and cover the cording
to make piping. With right sides
facing, sew the piping along the
seam line to the cross-stitched
piece; finish ends.
   With right sides together, sew
the front to back, leaving 4-inch
opening at top for turning. Clip
corners, turn and press. Stuff doll
with fiberfill and sew opening
closed.

   HAIR: For the bangs, wrap yarn
around a 2x5-inch strip of cardboard 28 times. Spread yarn to
measure 4½ inches; sew across
one long side only. Cut along other long side. Center and hand-sew
the sewn edge to the top of the
head along the seam line.
   For braids, wrap yarn around a
5x25-inch cardboard strip 36
times. Spread yarn at center to
measure 4½ inches and sew to
seam tape. Hand-sew center of
hair to center back of head. Pull
hair to sides of face and braid; tie
ends of braids with yarn. Tack
braids in place to sides of face.
Cut ribbon in half and tie in bows
to ends of braids.

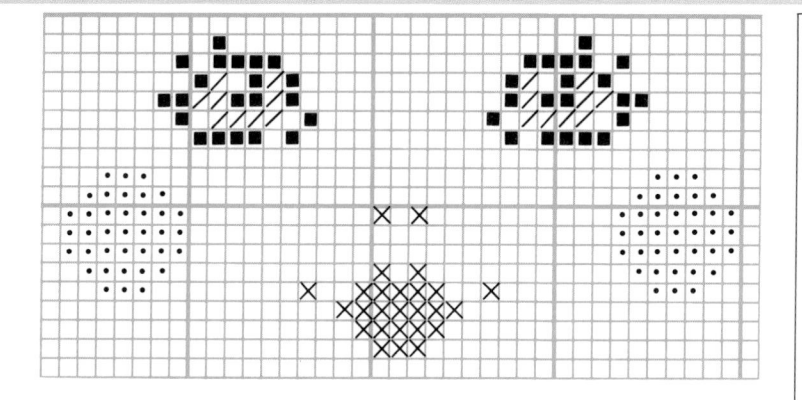

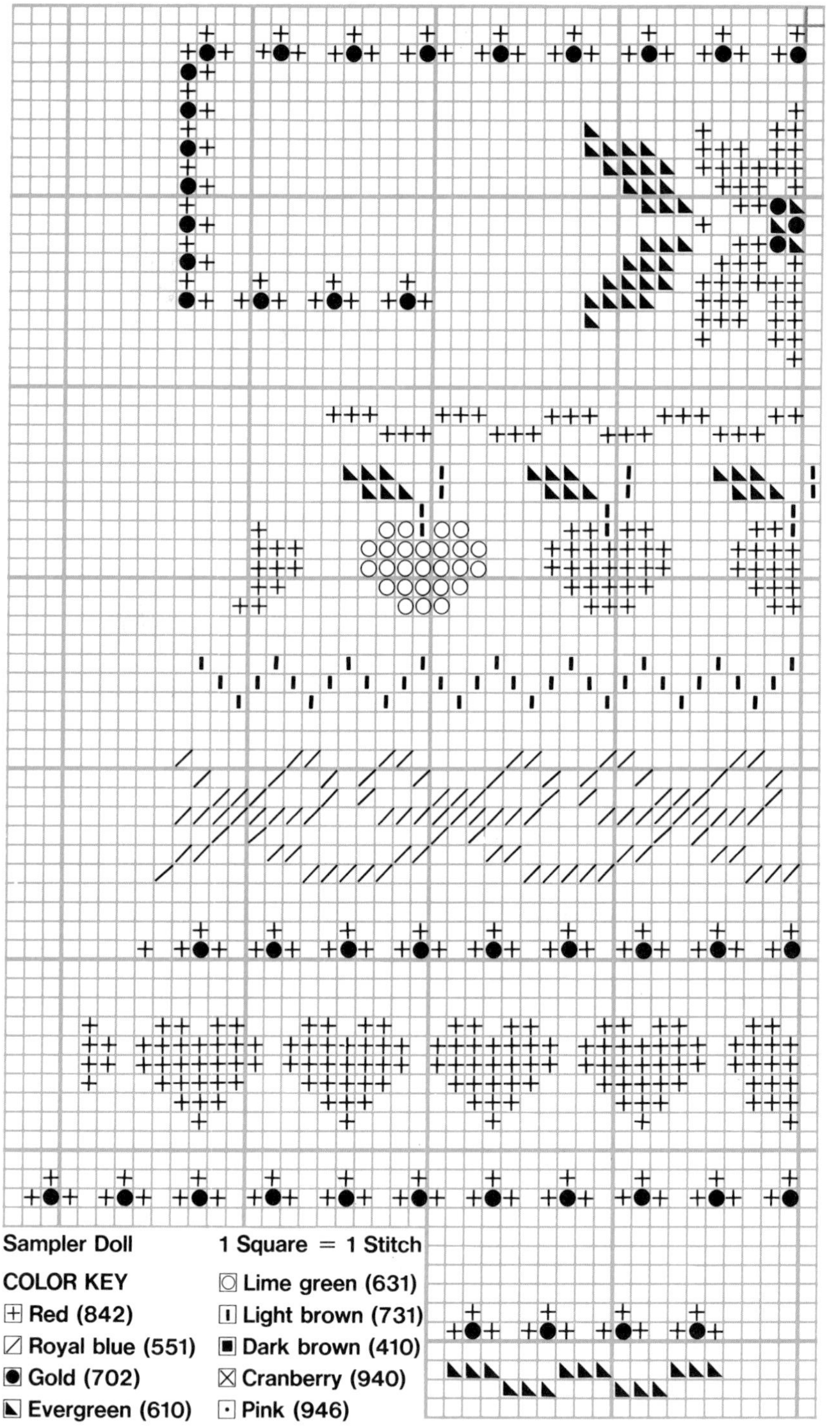

## Sampler Christmas Stockings

Shown on page 66.

Finished size of both stockings is 22½ inches tall.

**MATERIALS**
**To make one stocking**
16x26½-inch piece of 14-count Fiddler's cloth (available at needlecraft supply stores or by writing to Charles Craft, Inc. P.O. Box 1049, Laurinburg, NC 28352)
¾ yard of 44-inch-wide muslin for backing and lining
Polyester fleece for interfacing
2 yards of purchased red piping
Tracing paper
Water-erasable pen
**Stocking with the house motif**
Paternayan 3-ply Persian yarn in the following amounts and colors: 5 strands *each* of red (No. 841) and evergreen (No. 610); 3 strands of yellow (No. 760); 2 strands *each* of burgundy (No. 940), royal blue (No. 551), kelly green (No. 631), light blue (No. 553), and khaki brown (No. 454); and 1 strand of earth brown (No. 410)
**Stocking with the angel motif**
Paternayan 3-ply Persian yarn in the following amounts and colors: 5 strands of olive green (No. 612); 4 strands of red (No. 842); 3 strands *each* of gold (No. 702) and kelly green (No. 620); 2 strands *each* of light brown (No. 731), royal blue (No. 551), light blue (No. 552), federal blue (No. 501), gray (No. 200); and 1 strand *each* of dark brown (No. 430), and peach (No. 491)

**INSTRUCTIONS**
Before beginning, see the general information on pages 78 and 79 for special cross-stitch tips and techniques, and for materials necessary for working all counted cross-stitch projects.

*continued*

**Sampler Doll**     1 Square = 1 Stitch

**COLOR KEY**
⊞ Red (842)         ⊙ Lime green (631)
⧄ Royal blue (551)  ⊡ Light brown (731)
◉ Gold (702)        ◼ Dark brown (410)
◣ Evergreen (610)   ⊠ Cranberry (940)
                    ⊡ Pink (946)

# CHRISTMAS SAMPLER

STITCHING THE DESIGN: Referring to the charts, *far right*, select the stocking design of your choice and begin stitching the border along the top of the stocking 2 inches from *both* the top and right edge of the fabric. Use one ply of yarn to work the cross-stitches over two threads of the Aida cloth.

On the stocking with the house motif, work the poles and masts for sails on the ships with long stitches using dark brown.

On the stocking with the angel motif, backstitch the beaks of the birds with orange; use dark gray to make French knots for the birds' eyes.

When all cross-stitching is complete, zigzag ½ inch around shape on all sides; press.

ASSEMBLY: Enlarge and trace pattern for stocking, *opposite*, onto tracing paper; cut out stocking shape. Referring to the photo on page 66, carefully align the traced stocking atop the stitched piece. With the water-erasable pen, draw the stocking shape onto the fabric.

Cut stocking shape from Aida cloth, leaving ⅜-inch seam allowance. Cut another stocking piece from muslin and two more pieces from muslin for lining. Cut two fleece pieces to match.

Baste one fleece piece to wrong side of stitched piece and one to backing. With right sides facing, sew piping to the cross-stitched piece around all edges.

With right sides together, sew stocking backing to front, leaving top edge free. Clip curves, turn and press.

With right sides facing, sew remaining two muslin pieces together, leaving top edge free; trim seams. Press back ⅜-inch seam along top edge. Insert lining inside stocking and hand-sew lining atop piping seam along top of stocking.

**Sampler Stockings**

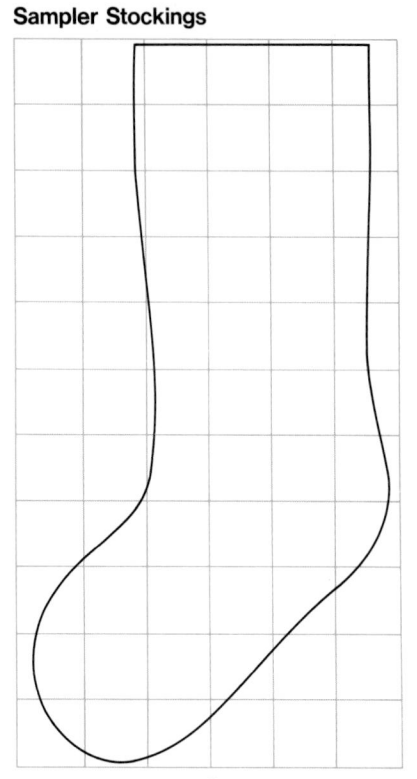

1 Square = 2 Inches

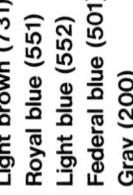
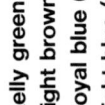
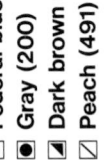

**Angel Stocking**
COLOR KEY

| | | |
|---|---|---|
| ⊡ Olive green (612) | ◨ Light brown (731) | ● Gray (200) |
| ◢ Red (842) | ◻ Royal blue (551) | ◣ Dark brown (430) |
| ⊠ Gold (702) | ⊟ Light blue (552) | ◿ Peach (491) |
| ⊟ Kelly green (620) | ⊞ Federal blue (501) | |

1 Square = 1 Stitch

**House Stocking**
COLOR KEY

| | | |
|---|---|---|
| ⊠ Red (841) | ◻ Royal blue (551) | ◻ Khaki brown (454) |
| ◢ Evergreen (610) | ⊡ Kelly green (631) | ⊟ Earth brown (410) |
| ◼ Yellow (760) | ● Light blue (553) | |
| ⊞ Burgundy (940) | | |

1 Square = 1 Stitch

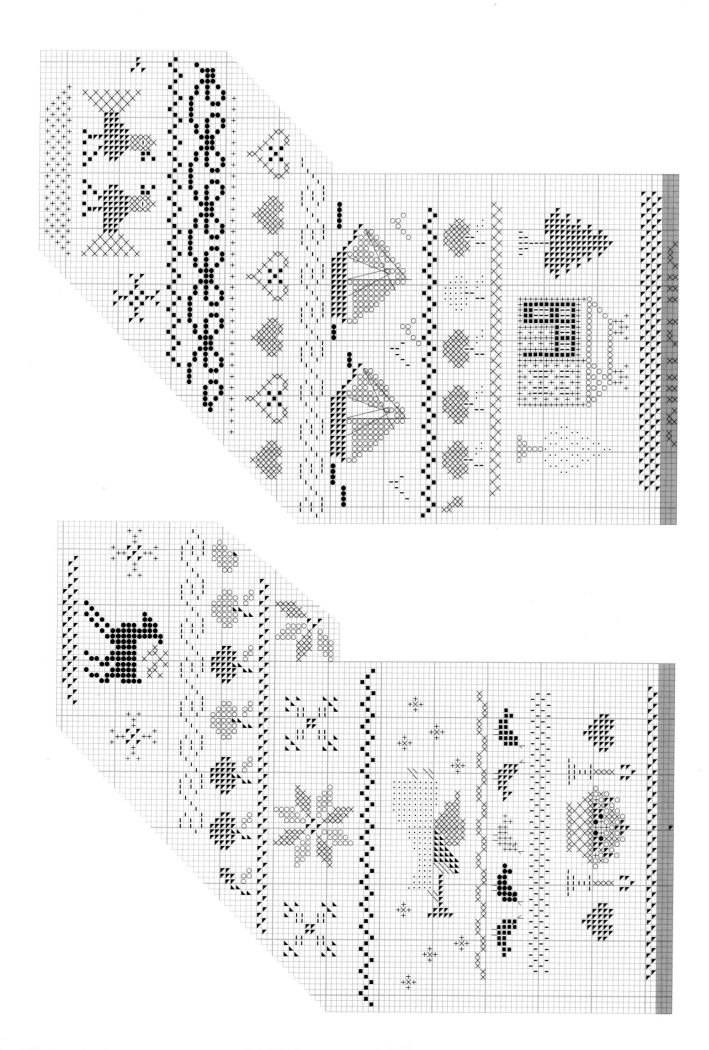

# TIPS AND TECHNIQUES

*Counted cross-stitch is a delightful craft, and one that's easy to master. Learn just one basic stitch, and the technique is at your fingertips!*

*To guide you through all the cross-stitching projects in this book, here are tips for selecting patterns, threads, fabrics, and needles, as well as finishing and blocking techniques.*

## Start with a Pattern

### Assemble pattern materials

Many of the designs in this book can be stitched directly from the charts. For some designs, however, we've included only a portion of the pattern (one half or one fourth, for example). These need to be charted onto graph paper so you have a complete chart to stitch from.

Before you begin, assemble the following materials and supplies: masking tape, graph paper, felt-tip marking pens or colored pencils, a ruler, pencils, mat knife, and scissors.

GRAPH PAPER: Graph paper comes in many grid sizes, such as 4, 10, and 14 squares to the inch. Because the grids in this book are marked in increments of 10, graph paper with 10 squares per inch probably is the easiest to use for charting.

Graph paper pads and sheets come in a variety of sizes as well. Select the size that best accommodates your design. If you have to piece sheets, carefully align the squares, then tape them together on the *reverse* side.

COLORED MARKERS: Gather pencils or felt-tip pens in shades that correspond to those on the color key for the pattern you intend to stitch.

### Working from a chart

Before beginning to stitch, it's important to start with a complete and accurate pattern. Cross-stitch patterns are charted on grids with special symbols that represent the colors of thread used for embroidery. Symbols are noted in the color key and accompany each pattern.

Look carefully at the pattern given in the book and locate the center of the *finished* design. Next, find the center of the graph paper. With a ruler and a pencil, draw horizontal and vertical lines on the graph paper, marking the center of the height and the center of the width, respectively.

Starting from this point, begin marking crosses with colored pens or pencils. Chart the diagram as it appears in the book, then flop the pattern, making one or more mirror images of the printed chart on your graph paper pattern.

If you make a mistake when charting the pattern, simply eliminate the mistake, using white typewriter correction fluid. If the error is over a large area, cut out the mistake with a mat knife and patch the hole with additional graph paper taped to the wrong side of the pattern.

## Choosing Materials

### Even-weave fabrics

You can work counted cross-stitches on many fabrics. Even-weave fabrics are the obvious choice, but by using waste canvas, you can work cross-stiches on many closely woven fabrics.

In even-weave fabrics, the vertical and horizontal threads are the same thickness throughout the cloth. Fabrics come in many colors and thread counts, allowing great flexibility in the size of the finished design.

HARDANGER CLOTH: This is one of the more common fabrics used for counted thread work. The thread count *always* is 22 threads per inch.

AIDA CLOTH: This cloth appears to be made of tiny squares and is a good choice for beginners, because the squares define the area for working each stitch. Aida cloth comes in many sizes— 6-, 8-, 11-, 14-, and 18-count.

NEEDLEPOINT CANVAS: Experiment with cross-stitches on needlepoint canvas, leaving the background unworked. It, too, is available in a variety of thread counts and colors.

WASTE CANVAS: Waste canvas is a special even-weave material that allows you to work counted cross-stitches atop fabrics other than even-weaves.

Stitches worked over waste-canvas look exactly like stitches worked on even-weave fabric. But waste canvas enables you to embroider on batiste, cotton, broadcloth, organdy, denim, gabardine, poplin, wool, and other tightly woven fabrics.

This canvas is available in sizes ranging from 6 to 16 squares per linear inch. The canvas can be pieced, but it is preferable to purchase an amount that covers the entire area to be stitched.

Lay canvas atop fabric, making sure the grid of the canvas is even with the grain of the fabric. Pin and baste the canvas in place.

To work the stitches, insert the threaded needle into the *smallest* squares of the canvas. Be careful not to catch the canvas when stitching; otherwise, removing the canvas threads will be difficult and stitches will be pulled out of shape.

When the stitching is complete, moisten canvas; pull out the horizontal threads, one at a time and in order. Then, pull the vertical threads until the canvas is completely removed.

## Yarns and Threads

### Select threads

Your choices of color and variety of thread and yarn are enormous. Here are some of the more traditional materials used for cross-stitch projects.

EMBROIDERY FLOSS: Six-strand floss is available in the widest range of colors of any thread. Flosses are available in 100 percent cotton, rayon, or silk. Whether you use one or all six strands for stitching will depend upon the fabric and number of threads each cross-stitch is worked over.

PEARL COTTON: Pearl cotton is available in three sizes—Nos. 3, 5, and 8. (No. 3 is thick; No. 8 is thin.) This floss has an obvious twist and a high sheen.

WOOL YARN: A single strand of three-ply wool gives a rich look to cross-stitches. Wool yarns work best on loosely woven fabrics.

### Working with threads

Cut thread into lengths that you find comfortable to work with (18 inches is a good length). However, cut unusual threads that fray easily—rayons, silks, or metallics—into shorter lengths for finer looking stitching. Knot the cut strands loosely together, and mark them with the appropriate color number.

## Types of Needles

### Distinguishing needle styles

Needles come in all shapes and sizes; they may be thick or thin, wide- or narrow-eyed, long or short, and sharp- or blunt-pointed. The needle you select depends upon the threads and fabrics used for your project.

TAPESTRY NEEDLES: Tapestry needles have long eyes for holding multiple plies of thread, but the end of the needle is blunt rather than sharp. Use these needles to stitch on mono needlepoint canvas, perforated paper, and even-weave fabrics because they will not catch or snag the materials.

EMBROIDERY NEEDLES: Also called crewel needles, embroidery needles have the long eye characteristic of tapestry needles, but also have a sharp point for stitching on fine woven fabrics. These needles are ideal when you work with embroidery flosses, Nos. 5 or 8 pearl cotton, metallic threads, or one ply of three-ply wool yarn.

CHENILLE NEEDLES: Chenille needles have the same qualities as embroidery needles, but they are available only in a larger range of sizes. Longer eyes make them ideal for crewel embroidery and for stitching with wool yarn or No. 8 pearl cotton.

## Stitching the Design

### Select a starting point

The point at which you begin to stitch varies with each design. Usually the center of the pattern is best, but beginning in a corner is appropriate if you are certain of the finished size of your project.

If you are working a sampler, allow extra fabric around the design for framing. You may wish to leave a border of plain fabric around the stitchery *before* framing, and you must allow excess fabric for stretching the stitchery around the backing material to staple to the framing strips.

Using masking tape, bind edges of the fabric to prevent raveling.

### Beginning and ending a stitch

The best way to begin a cross-stitch is by using a *waste knot*. It is a temporary knot and will be clipped later. To begin, knot the end of a threaded needle. Insert the needle into the right side of the fabric, about 4 inches away from placement of the first cross-stitch. Bring the needle up through the fabric and work the first series of cross-stitches. Stitch until the thread is used up or until the area to be filled with this color is complete.

To finish the thread, slip the threaded needle under the previously stitched threads on the wrong side of the fabric for 1 to 1½ inches. (You may wish to weave the thread back and forth a few times.) Clip the thread.

Turn the piece to the right side and clip the waste knot. Rethread the needle with the excess floss and push the needle to the wrong side of the stitchery. Fasten the thread as directed above.

### Working a cross-stitch

One completed cross-stitch is square. The number of threads of the fabric that a cross-stitch is worked over varies from project to project. (See project instructions.) The important points to remember are to make all stitches a uniform size, and to *work all the topstitches in the same direction*.

To make a cross-stitch, pull the threaded needle from the wrong side of the fabric through the appropriate hole in the even-weave fabric. Carry the needle across and up the appropriate number of threads and insert it in the upper right corner of the square.

The second part of the stitch begins in the lower right corner of the square. Bring the needle up through the fabric and carry it across the required number of threads, inserting it into the fabric at the upper left corner of the square, finishing the stitch.

### Maintain uniform stitches

When embroidering, always keep stitch tension uniform. If threads are pulled too taut, the fabric and stitches become distorted. If threads are too loose, the shape of the stitches is lost.

### Carrying threads

When working with areas that use a variety of thread colors, you need not end your thread every time you use a different color. Carry the thread across the back of the fabric, but, to secure the thread, slip the threaded needle under previously stitched crosses. If you carry the threads *loosely* to another area, without securing the thread, the piece can easily become distorted.

### Blocking the stitchery

Once you have completed the stitchery, remove the tape from the raw edges. Lay a thick cloth over your ironing board and place the stitchery right side down over the cloth. Dampen a pressing cloth and lay it atop the stitchery and press the piece using a moderately hot iron.

After blocking, the embroidery is ready for you to frame or assemble into your project.

# ACKNOWLEDGMENTS

*Our special thanks to the following designers who contributed projects to this book. When more than one project appears on a page, the acknowledgment specifically cites the project with the page number. A page number alone indicates one designer or source has contributed all of the project material listed for that page.*

Laura Holtorf Collins—40–41; 62–63
Dixie Falls—4–5; 20; 23, sampler
Diane Hayes—26; 36–37
Rebecca Jerdee—64–66, design adaptations
Juene Johnson for Cinnamon Rainbow—44–45
Beverly Rivers—42
Sara Jane Treinen—6–7, design adaptations; 8–9, design adaptations; 10, design adaptation; 24–25; 43, Santa bag design adaptation
Jim Williams—11; 22, design adaptation; 23, hearth stool design adaptation; 38–39; 67, design adaptation

*We also are pleased to acknowledge the following photographers, whose talents and technical skills contributed much to this book.*

Jim Hedrich—62–63, 64–65, 66–67
Thomas Hooper—22–23
Hopkins Associates—4–5, 6–7, 8–9, 10–11, 20–21, 24–25, 36–37, 38–39, 40–41, 42–43, 44–45
Scott Little—26–27

*For their creative skills, courtesy, and cooperation, we extend a special thanks to:*

Lu Ann Bagnall
Barbara Bergman
Gary Boling
Jackie Fees
Donna Glas
Kathy Ferguson
Nancy Helgeson
Dorothy Hohnbaum
Susan Knight
Chris Neubauer
Jil Severson
Margaret Sindelar

*For their cooperation and courtesy, we extend a special thanks to the following sources:*

Astor Place, Ltd.
239 Main Ave.
Stirling, NJ 07980

DMC Corporation
197 Trumbull St.
Elizabeth, NJ 07206

C.M. Offray & Son, Inc.
261 Madison Ave.
New York, NY 10016

Paternayan Yarns
Johnson Creative Arts
445 Main Street
West Townsend, MA 01474

Joan Toggit Ltd.
35 Fairfield Place
West Caldwell, NJ 07006